Julian Cundiff

CARP

Short Session Success

ANGLING PUBLICATIONS

First published in 2010

British Library Cataloguing in Publication Data

Carp – Short Session Success

Carp Angling
Angling Publications Ltd.

ISBN HB 1-871700-79-4
ISBN SB 1-871700 -78-7

Compiled, designed and produced by
Angling Publications Ltd.

Printed by MPG Books

Other Books by Julian Cundiff:

Carp Waters 1991
Practical Carp Fishing 1993
Successful Carp Fishing 1994
Beekay Guide To Starting Carping 1995
Beekay Guide To Carp Rigs 1996

Dedication

This book is dedicated to my family who continue to
support my journey through life and my many friends
who live it with me. Particular thanks go to Tim Paisley,
Kevin Nash and Kevin Maddocks for inspiration, and to Bill
Cottam and Richard Skidmore for always putting friendship
above business. Like anybody else there have been difficult
times in my life so to those who have lifted my spirits to
enable what you have in front of you to be written an
extra special thank you to you all.

Acknowledgements

I am very lucky in that I have been very well supported
over the years by a number of companies and to all those
a big thank you and I hope I have repaid your faith in me.
In particular, I would like to acknowledge those who have
allowed me to use the best products that are available in
carp fishing and make my pursuit of carp that much more
easier. I am not an angler who likes to chop and change
without good reason so if I write about it I do indeed use it
and probably have done so for many years.

To all at Antbait, John at C and M Eyewear, the team at
Daiwa, Dave at Drennan, Larry and Martin at Dynamite,
Chris at Enterprise, Paul and Lewis at Fox, Lewis at Gardner,
HBS and Hinders past and present, Ali, Adam and the boys
at Korda, Pete and Dave at Kryston, Keith, Alan and Nick
at Nash, Nutrabaits staff through the ages, Optilabs staff,
Jase and Howard at Rollin', Lee at the Tackle Box and
Simon at Wychwood.

Contents

Introduction

"Short session success is down to long term planning"....
so said a good friend of mine one day as we returned
yet another double on a day when most anglers would
have sat at home rather than tackle the difficulties of carp
fishing in winter. No doubt the anglers on the opposite bank
cocooned in their bivvies would be wondering just how
on earth we made it look so easy in the few hours we had
available to us but all will be revealed within the book you
have in your hands. If I make it sound easy it is because at
times it can be! Carp fishing is only as hard as you make
it and I hope by the time you get to the end of the book
you too will have the ability to make short sessions work
through a long-term approach and methodical thinking.

Mid July on a popular water, not untypical of the
type of water any of you can, and probably do, fish...

"It was an early finish at work and then down the
motorway to the water in question. Normally the venue
is one I only target in the winter and I was quite surprised
at just how pretty the water was in the summer. I was also
quite dismayed to see how popular it was with two out
of the three banks being lined with carp anglers, a real
change to the winter when mid week would generally
see it empty. However the furthest bank from the car park
was the one the wind was blowing into, and a strong one
as well looking at the bend on the trees above the swims.
I knew I only had till 8.00a.m. the next day to get the job
done so with the car locked the tackle was loaded on the
barrow and I was soon pushing it past bivvy after bivvy to
the far bank. The water had a reputation as a prolific water
in the winter so with it being summer I really expected to
catch – if that doesn't sound too arrogant or presumptuous?

So just in case it was a red letter day I wanted to have everything in place – that's two landing nets, camera on the non-stick, unhooking mat placed and so on… time to play.

That's carp number 31 and I'd really better pack up for work.

    The water has a two-rod rule so once tackled up I decided to fish one at 40 yards and one at 60 yards. In winter the carp seem to prefer the middle area but with the wind in my face I was pretty confident I'd find more at under 60 yards than beyond that range. Rods went out with two-bait stringers and no free offerings. I'd fish that way until I was sure that I was not only in the right swim but also in the right spots in the swim. Lines settled, bobbins on and so was the coffee in under 45 minutes. The first rod took an hour to go from first arriving in the car park and surprisingly it was the longer range one rather than the one at 40 yards. Two shots of each side on the remote and out it went again to the same spot. 30 minutes later and the same rod was away again and once again I took some pictures of the mid double. By mid evening the wind had dropped considerably and because I was already on six carp to the 60-yard rod and not one to the 40-yard one I decided to fish both at 60 yards, but about 10 yards apart.

I'd started to 'stick' out the odd 20mm free offering after each take. The hookbait being one out of the bag with trimmed edges to both release the attractors quickly and make ejection more difficult. The more I put out the quicker the runs came, so out went a further 3 kilos with the throwing stick. Talk about tennis elbow, I had throwing stick arm! No sooner was the bait in than the rods were off. Between landing fish, photographing them, and clipping on a new rig I was getting worn out – this is a young man's game a la BYCAC-style carping. Most of the fish were in the mid-double range and fought like tigers in and out of the water. I had a couple of two-rod tangles and was glad at times of the spare rod I'd brought which allowed me to get at least one rod out whilst unpicking the other two.

As the light started to fade the average size got bigger and late evening saw me land what I thought was a big carp, only to find a huge catfish in the net. It fought for over 30 minutes and looked like a cross between a giant tadpole, fat eel and giant pike… How big it weighed I've no idea as once I'd photographed it I wanted to get the carp rods back into play. That wasn't the end of the action

Never had a cat before and now I've had two before work!

as the runs continued all night long and as I finally wound in at 7.00a.m. I'd had 31 doubles, a catfish and four bream. I'd gone through 30 pre-tied rigs and all the bait I had. The clothes were sodden, the digital camera out of images to use and I still had work to go to. An amazing overnight session for sure..."

I guess there will be many of you reading that thinking "Wow, that's incredible but it's all right for him: I could never do that." Well stop right now and start believing in yourself. There is not a single thing I did on that 16-hour overnight session that the majority of the people reading this could not duplicate and even improve on. The water was one anybody can join and cost a lot less than a good night out on the town. The rigs were bog standard fluorocarbon to long shank hook with a bottom bait and two-bait stringer. The bait was one you can get from any tackle shop and although I am lucky in that I choose the tackle I want your own rod, reel and indication system would have done just the same job.
I slept under a brolly and I would say I had the 12th choice of swim when I turned up. Like many of you I'd been at work and had to go to work the next day... So tell me now why you too could not achieve, or maybe even better, that ? No reason, and after reading this book you can and I hope will do so. I promise you all you need is a little self belief, the tools of the trade, and the inspiration and ideas that I can give you in this book.

Kevin Maddocks' book 'Carp Fever' made me believe I could do it and I know that 'Short Session Success' will do the same for you if you truly want it to.

When I was in my formative years in carp fishing, and maybe for many years thereafter, I didn't have such self belief and tended to say to myself that I could do that if I had the time, money, water, rigs or whatever excuse I could come up with for not being successful. Well I was wrong as I now know that it is possible to be successful, especially on short sessions, providing you are prepared, logical and have some self belief. Now I am sure you could be forgiven for thinking that's all well and good but he's the guy who writes in all the magazines, does the books and knows all the secrets. Well it's important that as you read this book you can put into context the advice I give you with the type of person I am and the life I lead. You know my face but what about me? What have we got in common that makes me believe that you can do just as well?

Well like many of you I have a full time job: it's a five day week working 9.00a.m. to 5.00p.m. with some flexi-time, the odd Saturday court and evening meeting. Although I love my carp fishing I have a life outside of carp fishing with a partner, a house to look after and friends and family who are just as important as carp fishing, if not more so. I've had my ups and downs and having been carp fishing for over 25 years now have seen many come and many go. With my job and lifestyle in the summer months from March through to late October I try to do at least one overnighter a week, if not two. Occasionally I will have a day off mid week to extend or start a session early if I think I am in with a chance to maximise that time. In the winter it's weekends only with the odd day off mid week now and again if the weather is favourable and the venue ice free! Of course I am lucky in that I use what I consider the best tackle available, but the items I use and the baits I use are ones you can all get from any tackle shop. I have never used anything other than the baits you see in the shops and the rigs I write about in the magazines. The waters I fish range from syndicates that anyone can join to day ticket waters you read about in the weeklies and monthlies. In short I have nothing, and do nothing that anyone reading 'Short Session Success' cannot have or do for themselves. What I do have is self belief created simply by getting out there and doing it. Sometimes it works and sometimes it doesn't but I have learnt just as much from my failures as I have from my successes. There have been times when I have felt like crying and there have been times when I have had the red letter days we all dream of. In short, you and I are probably very similar and what I do you can do too.

Wherever my sessions are time and distance are always a priority.

Introduction

When I started to write this Introduction I really wanted to convey to you what this book and my fishing is all about. I once saw bait described as 'confidence in a bag', well that's what I want this book to be for you. At around 50,000 words it cannot hope to cover everything I know but I have included within the reference chapter a selected further reading guide that I know would be excellent additional material to have in your hands. I started carp fishing in the early 80s and the books I read then inspired me, but at times didn't have enough that I could 'duplicate to replicate' as they say. Well this is the book that I would have wanted to have available when I started, one that hopefully will both inspire, educate and motivate you to short session success. At the very end of the book I have included an address where you can contact me for any additional help. In this day and age it is near-impossible to claim that anything is a 'first', but such is my belief in the book that for the first time ever you will be able to write to the author if you need any additional information. Couple the book with the address and it's just like taking me carp fishing with you.

Enjoy the read, believe in yourself and I know that no matter what you want from carp fishing together we can achieve it.

Short Session Success… let the game begin.

Julian Cundiff
September 2010

Chapter One
Mind Games:
Take Me Fishing With You

Although there have been many excellent technical books on carp fishing published, I have noticed that little attention is placed on motivation or 'getting your mind into gear' as I call it. With the greatest respect to baits, rigs and venue choice if you are not there because you can't be bothered to go you are not going to catch them are you? And why do anglers not bother to go, or not do things properly when they are there? Because they are not motivated enough to do so! OK, occasionally anglers do make genuine mistakes through ignorance but compared to failure through lack of effort, that's not in the same ball park I assure you. I used to think carp could not 'really' be caught in the winter and instead used to fish for pike. Nowadays I know that carp can be caught in the winter and if I am not there it's because I didn't motivate myself to go. If I am there and not catching I really do ask myself why I am not catching? Is it the carp or is it that I am not trying hard enough? That, my friend, is down to your mind and your motivation. So before we start delving into venues, baits and rigs let's look at where you are with your fishing and how that will impact on the advice I give.

First of all take a look at yourself and what you want from your carp fishing in comparison to what you are getting from it. Yes I know a lot will depend on the venue you fish but the starting point for any angler is to look at their fishing and what they want from it. A short session is different things to different people and to an angler who fishes every weekend a short session may well be anything less than a weekend, say maybe a 24-hour session? But for an angler like me who only gets the chance to do an overnighter, or a full day at the most, a short session could be an evening. Although all the carp fishing magazines, DVDs , television coverage and internet are great for

Set up in the pouring rain and it was worth it.

information purposes they can confuse, bewilder and over-complicate things at times. There is an old expression which said that 'ignorance is bliss' and to a large extent it is. Sometimes the more you know the worse it gets and you can end up not seeing the wood for the trees. Pictures of anglers holding carp in magazines may well inspire but I know that when things are not going to plan they can also confuse. Do you really know what time and effort that person put in to catch that carp? A catch report in Carp-Talk does not tell the full story, and even a magazine feature often cannot convey the effort put in. Luck may well have a part in carp fishing but I am a great believer in making your own luck, riding it when it works and getting on with it when it does not.

So first job is to stop and think about where you are and where you want to be. Forget what others are doing or not doing and concentrate on yourself and what you want out of it. Your carp fishing is all that should matter to you, not what others have caught or not caught. If they are on the same water as you then they can be a useful reference point as to how you are or are not doing but other than that… be realistic and not bewildered. I look at many magazines that are out and at times I too start to think I am getting it wrong, but then I employ a little tactic that I call 'self correcting'. I say to myself 'GET A GRIP' and concentrate on your own fishing Jules. Anglers such as

Most articles, mine included, concentrate on the technical not mental side of things.

Terry Hearn, Dave Lane, Jim Shelley are probably to many of you what anglers like Kevin Maddocks, Andy Little and Rod Hutchinson were to me. I used to believe that they had something that I didn't have, be it venues, rigs, baits and so on. Having fished with them and knowing them I now know that providing I apply myself correctly I can be as successful as I can be for the effort that I put in, but at the same time it has to be said that I could no more be the next Kevin Maddocks or Andy Little than you will be the next Terry Hearn or Dave Lane. So forget about what others are doing other than in a 'learning from' sense. Whether you fish a water full of singles or doubles, 20s or even 30s, concentrate on you and you alone. You will learn far more from the successful angler on that water than you will ever learn from a 'name' in the press who is not fishing your water. Don't get me wrong, I am amazed and inspired at what these guys do but when it comes to being successful on my waters I have learnt a lot more from the local lads doing well to the left and right of me than I have ever learnt from the capture of a big carp from another water miles away from me. Inspiration is one thing but education to success on short sessions is a different thing.

On my overnighters I can't leave anything to chance.

Carp-Talk publishes the pictures but doesn't always describe the hard work behind the captures.

Although you may not realise it your mind is the best asset you have. Your alarm clock may well go off at

Two of my inspirations – Rod Hutchinson and Mike Wilson. But whilst they have inspired me, I still need to do the hard work myself.

A freezing cold morning and the lake was starting to ice up. I moved three times and still blanked. Would you have the drive to keep doing it?

5.00a.m. on a cold January morning but it is your mind and motivation that makes you swing your legs out of bed to complete the process of getting up. Hi-attract baits and razor-sharp hooks may well do the trick when cast to the right spot but if you are lazy and can't be bothered to look for them in the first place they are not going to be much use if you are a 100 yards from the nearest carp. If your mind is sorted you will be motivated to do things and, most importantly to do them well, which is what counts on short sessions. So before you read the rest of the book and start applying for permits, buying new bait and tying new rigs stop and think. What do I want from my fishing and what am I prepared to do to achieve it?

A long time ago, having spent some seasons targeting the biggest fish in local waters and eventually having caught those target fish, I realised that at that time, and at this time, I am not motivated enough by big fish in the same way that some anglers are. I am motivated to go fishing for carp between 10 and 35lb, coupled with what I consider to be a balanced life, and then I try my hardest in the time available. Because I am not driven to pursue target 'big fish' I could never do the weekend hike down to the circuit waters you may have read about.

A January double - one of a dozen that day when the lake was almost frozen.

However, nobody is as motivated as me to do well on the waters that I do choose to fish. I will get up in the middle of the night in winter. I will recast in the pouring rain. I will move swims if I see a fish. I will tie rigs up in advance, and so on. Short session carp fishing when it comes to motivation is really no different to targeting big carp. How much you want to catch the fish will equate to the effort you put in. You are yourself and nobody else... That sounds obvious but many carp anglers neglect that simple fact. You are where you are and you have the time and finances that you have. How you make that work for you is up to you. Once you accept that and start to build round it then it will come right. I live in the north of England and although there are waters with big fish present, if I was living in the south of England the fish I would be targeting would probably be a lot bigger. That said there would be more pressure on those fish and so on. I am where I am and I am motivated to try as hard as I can at the venues I choose in the time I make available for it. In that sense I am no different to you in that all things being equal success or failure is down to me. If I spent less time in the gym, socialising at weekends or writing articles I would have more time to fish for carp and may catch more. That said a balance in life is what works for me so I live with

There is more to life than fishing. KISS at Download was magnificent... two nights later I was fishing again!

the time I have. I benefit from my life outside carp fishing but I try as hard as I can when I am there and in the preparations I put in beforehand.

I am honest with myself (although maybe not at the time when I am smarting from a blank or lost fish!) and accept that usually lack of success is down to not putting quite enough effort into that session. Even now I still make mistakes by not moving, not recasting or not trying a different tactic. I know it's not the carp that are letting me down but me getting it wrong. If you learn to accept your own failings you will learn to be able to correct them. If your approach to carp fishing is 'it's all right for him but...' then stop right now and think. You alone have the ability to make short session carping work for you. If you are expecting unrealistic results from the time you have available you are going to end up very disappointed. You either need to create more time or be more realistic in your expectations. Once you can accept this you will end up wasting less of your energy worrying and moaning and will be able to channel that energy into making the short sessions work for you.

What can you expect from short sessions? Well that depends on you but go back to the introduction I wrote and look at who I am, where I am and what I do. Two years in a row I caught over forty 20lb carp in a year on overnighters. I have had over a 100 doubles in a winter yet had to travel nearly three hours to each venue at the time. I had numerous 30s and 20s yet never fished more than two overnighters a week that year. That's not bragging it's simply saying to you that success or failure is in your hands. What controls those hands is your mind and how motivated you are to try as hard as you can. I can tell you the rigs and baits to use but I can't make you

Working for the court system pays the bills but reduces my fishing time, so I have to get my mind around the time I do have available.

tie them properly. I can tell you about the benefits of being first there and last to leave but I can't make you get out of bed to do that. I can tell you about the need to watch for fish in the dark but I can't make you leave the books and DVD player at home. Only you can do that and only you will do that when it matters to you.

I was absolutely shattered after a day at work, but stood out in the pitch black listening for the sounds of carp rolling.

Does it matter to you? Well I hope so because you are reading this book. If you accept that you can do better and will do better your mind is in the right place to start with. Often the anglers who are least successful are the ones who think they have least to learn. Ignorance is not bliss but it's certainly a good self-defence mechanism for some. I know you can do it but if you want to be successful on the short sessions sort that mindset out, be clear in your journey and you will succeed. Whether you have only a few hours or 24 hours matters not. What does matter is the effort you put in. If you are motivated the rest will come I promise you.

Chapter Two
Choose the Right Water

I am sure there will be some of you who have, or feel they have, the ideal water for short session carping already. To those of you I say don't skip this one as you never know. If you really sit and think about it, it may be that you are limiting your chances of success by perhaps not being on quite the right water no matter how good it feels at the moment. Make no mistake if your time is limited getting on the right water can be the difference between consistent success and heartbreaking failure. Take it from me the guys who you see week in week out in the press are not just good carp anglers but they are good carp anglers fishing the right waters. Sometimes you can be a proficient carp angler and simply not be in a position to put your own ability to good effect. For years I really struggled with my winter carping in the north of England but when I started to travel to places like Willow Park in Surrey, Catch 22 in Norfolk and Messingham Sands in Lincolnshire my catch rate went through the roof because I was on prolific winter waters. The same applied in summer and when I moved on to places like Three Lakes and Tilery I caught 20-pounders, not because I had greatly improved as a carp angler but because those waters had a better stock of big fish that responded to my short session tactics.

There are a number of considerations when it comes to choosing the right water and I suppose a lot depends on you and your lifestyle and targets. However, the first area to look at is the time you have available to you. I will be looking at how to make the best of the time you have but I am sure you are more than aware of generally what time you can set aside for carp fishing. For many I would think the week is taken up with work and so fishing is either weekends or overnighters, or maybe a few hours snatched before or after work. Be honest with yourself and look at what time you realistically have as sometimes you will have to balance desire (i.e. the ideal water) with reality (i.e. the time you can put into it).

Secondly, you have to consider what are the characteristics that you seek in a water bearing in mind the time you have to fish it. Again there are different things that appeal to us but the ones that do seem to crop up time and time again are as follows:

Day ticket or syndicate? I have permits for all types of venues and each have their pluses and minuses.

Size Be realistic as to what size of carp are you looking for. You need to consider not only the largest fish you are hoping to catch but the average size of the fish. Sometimes it is better to target a water with a higher average size of fish than a water that has a few big fish and few back up ones.

Numbers Although it sounds contradictory sometimes you really don't want too prolific a water if your sessions are overnighters and you are then going to work. The session I included in the introduction chapter was great for a one-off in the summer, or days in winter, but as a main target water nine months of the year it would probably kill me. So waters stuffed full of carp may well be OK to get a bend in the rod but in the time you have available are they going to be too prolific and lose their attraction pretty quickly? If you really do have very limited time such a water may be ideal.

With satellite navigation you can find out exactly how far a water is away from your home.

Cost Many readers will have to weigh up not only the cost of the permit but also the cost of fuel travelling to and from the water, taking into account the time you will be spending there. On a prolific water you will no doubt spend a lot more on consumables like bait, end tackle items and so on. Less action can equal less expense but too prolific a water can hit you financially. If it's a day ticket water consider how many sessions you will be doing and the overall cost. If it's a syndicate you need to divide the permit price by how many times you can get down there. Don't join then think!

Proximity The closer it is to home the more time you can spend fishing it, a simple statement but one that always plays a part in my water choice. In the spring to late autumn period I will be doing overnighters so my water will have to be no more than 30 to 60 minutes from where I keep my tackle. So I am looking for a water no more than 40 miles from my base. Even when you are not actually fishing the closer the water is the more chance you have of being able to pop in and keep tabs on it. And the closer it is the less fuel you use.

Aesthetics Even if all the above criteria are met the last and probably most important question is – do you like fishing there? If it's somewhere you just don't like being at then motivating yourself in the more difficult times is going to be a lot harder. If it's simply fish size that counts it can be possible to ignore your surroundings and fixate yourself on the target fish. However for many of you reading this you will also need to enjoy being there. If it's too popular it can be a lottery getting a swim and on short sessions

you are starting well behind the starting line. However for some anglers if it really is untapped and has no other anglers present when you are there that might be too quiet! Remember it's what YOU want not what other people think. I will only target waters where I have a realistic chance of getting on fish rather than constantly making the best of what is left. That to me is too much me against the angler than me against the carp.

> So those are just a few of the considerations I would suggest you take into account when considering a venue that's right for you. So how do you find that venue?

Word of mouth Probably the most common way to hear about a venue is from the time-honoured jungle telegraph. Providing it is direct from the person fishing the water and not the old 'someone knows someone who knows someone etc…' that is a great way to find out about waters. No doubt if you are reading this you do know other anglers and if they are friends then if they have fished the water it may well be worth looking into.

I really have to enjoy being there but what matters to you is what counts.

Local fishing tackle shops Especially if they are carp orientated or have a member of staff who is a carp angler. It is in the tackle shop's interests to get you out there and catching so they can get you back in for more spending.

Often you will see cards or notices displayed in the shop about local waters so ask those in the shop if they know of them or even better, fished them. Some shops have pictures of fish on the walls from local venues so once again ask and research.

Carp fishing magazines A great starting point is the weekly carp magazine Carp Talk. Not only does it have catch reports in it but catch reports from your local region and the details of the regional reporter who compiles the reports. You can soon find out more by giving them a call but please use your common sense and only contact them at sociable hours if you want a positive response! Crafty Carper has an excellent feature on day ticket waters so pick that up each month for contact details. This is part of the 'Ticketmaster' series and if you log onto the Angling Publications website you can download details of over 50 waters that may suit you. Carpworld has a long running series by Simon Crow entitled 'Open Access Waters' which is a comprehensive look at a different day ticket or open ticket water each

month. The series covers numerous waters and not only covers the fish but also the swims, history and contact details, so it's ideal. Add to these three the other weeklies and other carp fishing monthlies, and there really is no excuse not to have a starting point for that search for your ideal water.

The internet This really has come to the fore in recent years and if you look at some of the sites I have included in my reference chapter, whether you are from Sunderland or Staines a site will have waters for you to read about. Not only are there the major carp fishing sites but you can always do a Google search for waters around your home.

Carp slide shows and conferences

Although the Carp Society does not have the regional set up that it was once famous for its place in that aspect has been filled by many local carp meetings organised by local anglers, tackle shops or study groups. These tend to take place from November to March each year and you can find details in local tackle shops or on the numerous carp forums that exist. Not only will you get to see a speaker talk about carp fishing but often it can be a local lad: if you are courteous many will point you in the right direction. There are also a number of high-profile carp shows each year with the Carpin 'On two-day show being probably the best. There are numerous speakers at the show and you will be able to find out about waters countrywide. The Carp Society has its own two day conference each November which attracts many visitors and numerous stands which may help you in your search.

Take a trip to the famous Carpin On' show at 5-Lakes and you will pick up some great advice on waters and their suitability for you.

These are all possible starting points in the search for your ideal short session venue. In advance you should have made a checklist of what you do and do not want from a water, and with a number of waters to go at it is vitally important that you visit them at least once in advance no matter how good the information you have on them is and no matter how good it sounds. As we are looking at short session carping it's likely that the venue will not be too far away so a trip or two in advance is never wasted time: if anything it can prove a lot more productive than taking the fishing tackle with you.

At this stage you are not looking at how to fish at that water but IF that water is right for you ? Most waters will allow you to visit in advance and if not I would be dubious of the water – unless it is a particularly exclusive syndicate water. Always get permission first, or at least be certain that you can visit it to have a look. On your first visit turn up at a reasonable time, not pre-dawn which probably wouldn't endear you to the anglers on the venue

Not massive but once I found a productive winter water I upped my game.

that day. You will hopefully have some information about the water from your earlier research and now is the chance to see if the information is right and, more importantly, if the waters suits you. I would advise that you to go on your own, too; turning up with a mate or mates sometimes comes across as 'here's another load of keenies', whereas one lad on his own can come across as 'he seemed OK'. The trick is to be personable, not arrogant or over-inquisitive, and use your commonsense at all times. Watch and observe rather than question and give opinions. See if what you have already read and/or been told matches what you see at the water or can pick up from the locals.

If it's reputed to be prolific I would expect to see carp being caught during the visit. Anglers nowadays are often (quite rightly) proud of what they've caught and will usually be keen to tell you of their successes. Be gracious and avoid wearing clothing which shows allegiance to a particular bait firm as it may not be the chosen bait firm

of the guys you want help from. The majority of times I
have visited a 'prospective' water in advance I have soon
been able to weigh up whether it's for me or not. A couple
were ruled out due to their proximity to a motorway and
railway line and one was ruled out as it also doubled up as
a sailing club and jet ski club as well. All you need to do is
use your commonsense. Once you've made that first visit
you can usually tell but sometimes a second trip at dawn
or dusk is not a bad idea to see if the carp are showing at
these two prime times.

Does the water tick the right boxes for you? Does it
seem to be all it is claimed to be? Well if it is and you get
that 'just seems right' feeling then join, or at least be aware
of how you can join and the rules you will need to fish
to. Later on in the book I am going to look at winter carp
fishing to which the same rules apply, but perhaps with a
greater need to verify its winter pedigree. Venue sorted?
Great, let's move on and see how to make the most of the
time you have or can create for carp fishing.

Chapter Three
Time: Make The Most Of It

W ell, you've chosen the right water for your short session carping so what next? Load the car and get fishing that's what! Well you could but that's probably not the best way to get it right as soon as possible. Just hold back a little and let's look at how to make the most of your time so that even on the shortest of sessions you really are giving yourself the best chance. And I don't mean simply giving you advice on how to get the rods out as soon as possible, rather it is giving some pointers on creating and maximising your time.

I would hope that as you read this book you will realise that I try to look at all aspects of my carp fishing logically, and although carp can sometimes seem to do the most illogical of things, I do find the more logical your approach the better the result. Luck, yes it plays a part but the harder you work the luckier you will get!

The water has been chosen so now let's have a look at what makes you tick as a person. I don't mean you need to do anything in depth but what you need to do is have a clear idea of how important this short session carp fishing thing is to you to create as much time as possible. We are all different and some of you will be working and some of you won't. Some will work shifts and some nine to five. Some will have families and some will be single, or have a partner. Some of you will have carp fishing as your sole hobby whilst for others it may be one of many interests. This is where you need to start looking at just how important carp fishing is to you in comparison to all the other factors in your life. For example, I am a lawyer for the courts and, although I have a degree of flexi-time to play with; it's a five-day week, nine to five, so that is my first priority. I have my own home to run and a partner and parents and friends. I have all the responsibilities that go with writing and sponsorship. So those have to be met and my carp fishing then has to fit round that. Additionally I love weight training, motorbikes, watching motorsport and just relaxing, walking and chilling. That has to then fit round my carp fishing. Can you see the difference? My carp fishing fits round what I call the 'musts' in my life, but the second lot of interests which I call my 'luxuries' have to fit round my carp fishing. If I gave everything the same priority, or no priority at all, I would be all over the place and nothing would get done. So although it's not something I see written about start to get your life in order to find out what real time you can or want to devote to your short session carping.

It may be that what little time you thought you had can actually be improved on. We all only have twenty four hours a day to juggle with but when you start to look at what you can and can't cut back on sometimes you may surprise yourself on the time that really is available if it's important to you. The vital things you really can't cut back on and if you are employed then don't compromise your work situation. That is the rock behind your finances and without money it can be very hard to fish effectively. However, how much do you need to work and when? I could do a lot more Saturday courts but instead choose to let others do those so I have more time to myself to recharge my batteries, especially when I am doing a couple of overnighters mid week. However, I do have to do some so I tend to do these in the summer period so that in the colder months, when I like to do days for the best chance of a winter carp, I don't have to be sitting in court on a Saturday. Likewise,

Top **There is more to life than carp fishing. Despite seeing KISS three times on the Sonic Boom Tour I still fished and caught by managing my time as best I could.**

Family are important and are a definite 'must' in my life.

The water held carp to low 30s so I was never going to catch a PB, but at the time it was the best choice.

with flexi-time I try to build it up mid week in the winter so I can have the odd Friday or Monday off for longer sessions, or an extra one when a window of opportunity arises. In the summer I don't work late as I really want to be off a soon as possible to get to the water. What could you do to create some more time for yourself? If you are in education again you cannot compromise on that as that will not only affect the 'here and now' but potentially a big part of the rest of your life. When it comes to relationships if they are important then don't let carp fishing destroy them. I am lucky in that I have never been married and any breakdowns in my relationships were down to 'wrong choices' as Tim Paisley puts it. You have to decide what is important to you, what time they deserve and how you could live without them? Many carp anglers have fallen foul of this and no amount of carp are worth it if the relationship is important. Use your commonsense and try to look at it from their perspective. By all means give it your all but not at the wrong cost.

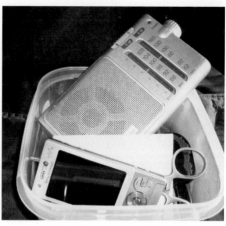

Football I can take or leave, but with the World Cup on I knew the waters would be quiet. I fished in relative peace and took the radio to keep up to date.

When it comes to what I deem the 'luxuries' time becomes a little easier to 'create', be it the pub, football or whatever else you choose to do while you are not carp fishing. In my case I love watching motorsport but it has a place and that place is Sky+, watched later in the evening so it doesn't interfere with our weekends. If I am doing two overnighters a week and then I am watching F1, Moto GP etc., I am in danger of kicking the you-know-what out of it. I'd love to carp fish more, and I could carp fish more, but some of my luxuries have to be included in my life so that I do not fall out of balance. But what works for me may not work for you, but not until you really sit down, think and plan can you decide that. Once you do that then the time you have left you truly can devote to getting it right on your short session carping.

Having made that decision it is important to look at your time on both a short and long-term basis. If it is local carp fishing then you can probably look at it more long term. You are probably going to be able to go more often and can pick things up as you go along. That's no excuse for turning up anything less than 100% prepared, but there is always another day. When you are travelling further afield you won't be able to go as often so it's a lot more short term and you have got to get it right. When I fished Catch 22 I knew that because it was almost 200 miles away I was only going to get in half a dozen trips during the winter so I created as much time as possible by always going on a Friday to give me maximum time to learn, adapt and benefit. However, the Selby Syndicate is only 30 minutes from home so shorter sessions were fine until I found a pattern I could exploit. That involved longer term planning with my time but both were equally important in their own way to get right.

You've got the water fixed and now you will have looked at what is and isn't important in your life time-wise. What next? Well it's a simple thing but what is the quickest way to get to your water? The sooner you are there the sooner you are looking, locating and hopefully banking those fish. In this day of the Satellite Navigation System and AA Autoroute it's a lot easier than maps and suchlike but sometimes you have to use commonsense as well. I know that on some venues that if I do not leave work by 3.00p.m. I will hit traffic and I will be delayed and end up there not much earlier than if I had left at 5.00p.m. And, worse still, I would have wasted flexi-time and got stressed up in the car in traffic. In my case when I am at a distant court one day I won't do an overnighter

This water saw very little pressure for years and getting there before first light meant I could always find the fish and get on them, even in the winter.

but I will if I am at a more local court. I do know the shortcuts and quickest routes so this buys me time, and time equals carp. I also look carefully at what are the best days to go or, more realistically, the best days not to go. You can never truly know this in advance on a new water but unless it is a very busy day ticket water you can soon start to pick up patterns as to when not to go. On some of my club waters where I like to do my overnighters I know that any lads taking a week off work will go on a Monday so I tend to avoid that day. Similarly if lads are looking for a long weekend they take Friday off work and go Thursday night so that's avoided. On many waters the Tuesday and Wednesday nights are the best for this very reason, or maybe even Sunday although I will look at this

Keeping healthy is a must in my book, it keeps me feeling motivated for the times when catching is a struggle and finding an excuse not to go is easy.

a little more in the overnighter chapter. The point is that with the greatest of respect to fellow anglers the fewer of them there are on the water the better, so the more times I can plan my time around their absence the better. You won't get it right all the time but if you don't think about it you are leaving it to chance and chance is not a friend of the short session carper.

Similarly you need to consider when it is best to put in your maximum effort. With the abolition of the close season and the slowing down of winter carp fishing many lads seem to stop carp fishing in November but go at it all guns blazing from March onwards. At one time the March to May period was very productive but if that is a time when your water has a huge influx of angler pressure you really need to consider your time management. Is it worth saving your holiday time to later in the year when some of the other anglers have burnt out? Is it worth going before the first mad rush? Making the most of the time you have is so important. Again, when we come to the chapters on spring, summer and winter I will look at how to maximise your time and results during those periods.

Weight training fits around my carp fishing and luckily I have a gym at home which means I can train day or night not just when the local gym is open.

No matter what water you fish it will have something in common with all the other waters in this country. It will have a dawn and dusk and invariably those periods are the most productive for observing and catching carp. Clearly you have to keep to the rules of the fishery and if it's a day ticket that only allows fishing from a set starting time to a set finishing time then that's your limit, but you still need to maximise that time. No matter what it takes you must be first in the queue to get there and last out of the gate at night. I have fished a number of such waters and if it's a 7.00a.m. start I would never be there any later than 6.00a.m., providing it was possible to do that. I hate getting up early but if I have to get up at 4.00a.m. to be first in the queue that's what I will do. I know that at Catch 22 when I fished there most lads would roll up Friday morning at around 9.00a.m. for their weekend stint. I would get up at 4.00a.m. and drive for three hours so that I was there for 7.00a.m. Similarly at Messingham Sands in the winter most lads arrive at around 7.00a.m. so I get up at 4.00a.m. to be there around 5.30a.m. I still only have a similar amount of time to fish but quite often I am where the fish are not just sitting in a swim that's left. When it comes to dusk I have noticed that on many waters if it's been a hard day many anglers pack up just into dark if they are not doing the full night. Just by hanging on an extra hour into dark results can be phenomenal. Make creative use of your time and hopefully not at a cost to you, your job or relationship.

Short session carping is so much more than just getting your rods out as soon as possible. If you take a step back, prioritise and combine these ideas with the specifics I detail in later chapters your short sessions may just be a little longer than you thought – and a lot more successful.

YORK RC

PUBLISHED ON: 2.7.10   THE MASTER COPY *MUST* BE CHEC

Day/Date	Ct. No.	At	Morning	Clerk	Afternoon	Clerk
Mon.	1	Y	REMAND	GM	REMAND	GM
	2	Y	ADULT TRIALS	JF	ADULT TRIALS	JF
5.7.10	3	Y	ADULT DCW	JC	ADULT DCW	DF
	4	Y	CASE PROGRESSION MEETING			DF am
	1	S	YOUTH TRIAL - Perry (Day 1 of 2)			ES
	2	S	FAMILY (Day 1 of 3)			EH
Tues.	1	Y	ADULT REMAND	JC	DV	JC
	2	Y	YOUTH TRIAL – Perry (Day 2 of 2)			ES
6.7.10	3	Y	YOUTH	GM	YOUTH Narey	GM
	4	Y	FAMILY (Day 2 of 3)			EH
	1	S	ADULT TRIALS	DF	ADULT TRIALS	DF
	2	S	NON CPS	DJ		DJ
Wed.	1	Y	REMAND/Narey	DF	REMAND/Narey	DF
	2	Y	ADULT TRIAL - ENSBURY (Day 1 of 2)			JF
7.7.10	3	Y	FAMILY (Day 3 of 3)			EH
	4	Y				
	1	S	ADULT TRIAL	GM	ADULT TRIAL	GM
	2	S	ADULT DCW	JC	ADULT DCW	JC
Thurs.	1	Y	REMAND	GM	REMAND	GM
	2	Y	ADULT TRIAL - ENSBURY (Day 2 of 2)			JF
8.7.10	3	Y	NON CPS	JC	NON CPS	JC
	4	Y	ADULT TRIALS	DJ	ADULT TRIALS	DJ
	1	S	ADULT TRIALS	ES	ADULT TRIALS	ES
	2	S	AD DCW/Narey	EH	Narey/DV	EH
Fri.	1	Y	REMAND/Narey	JF	REMAND/Narey	JF
	2	Y	ADULT TRIALS	EH	ADULT TRIALS	EH
9.7.10	3	Y				
	4	Y	BREACH	ES		
	1	S	ADULT TRIALS	JC	ADULT TRIALS	JC
	2	S				
	1	Y	PRISONERS	GM		

Class Ticket Type
STD ANYTIME DAY R   Adult ONE   Child NIL   OUT
Start date 29·JUN·10   Number 94988   4717641742
From DONCASTER
To YORK   Valid until 29·JUN·10   Price £14·30X
Route ANY PERMITTED   Validity ON DATE SHOWN
2-PART RETURN
Printed 87-58 on 29-JUN-10

Top Carp fishing has to fit around work and when the rota is done I work out which days are best suited to my overnighters.

Usually I drive but when I am tired I do indeed 'let the train take the strain'.

Chapter Four
Observe, Locate, Succeed

P utting the right rig with the right bait to the right spot at the right time can very much be a game of chance but providing you think about what you are doing, and play the percentage game to your advantage you can swing the odds your way. Yes you may well get lucky with a cast 'anywhere' but at the end of the day when it comes to short session carping the more time that bait is in front of the fish the better chance you have of catching. Whilst a long session angler may well be able to play the waiting game and hope that the fish come across the hookbaits, with the time you have you may be long gone by the time they visit your hookbait, if they visit it at all. So you need to choose the right swim – which I will cover in the next chapter – by observing and locating the carp, an aspect I am going to cover in this chapter. Observation is making sure that you are prepared and able to find the fish, and location is the art of finding them. I don't intend to cover how to plumb a swim for depth and features as – vital though the subject is – it really has been covered extensively in books and DVDs for years: if you turn to the reference chapter at the end of the book there is some recommended additional reading and viewing on this subject. 'Leading' a water to feel the nature of the swim is a whole different matter and you will find this in the chapter on accuracy.

Observation
The importance of eyesight: whilst you may well be able to locate carp through using your ears for sounds of carp crashing most observation is carried out using your eyes in conjunction with your brain. Now I cannot stress this too highly but the better your eyesight the better your chances of seeing the fish, or the tell-tale signs carp can give. As we get older our eyesight will inevitably fail and

Observe, Locate, Succeed

what was crisp and in focus can soon turn a little fuzzy round the edges. Unless you know that you have 20/20 vision do your own carp fishing chances a big favour and go and get your eyes tested. Many opticians will do free eye tests so that you can know for sure. For years I was short sighted and although it was not too bad in the day, at half light I really did struggle. And we all know that carp do love to show themselves in the half light of dawn and dusk. Boy oh boy, did I miss out on a lot of obvious signs! And as well as not being able to see them clearly the accuracy of casting and baiting suffers too. Once I had that eye test I knew I needed to get my eyes sorted as it was a part of carp fishing that I was not good at. Is it one of your strengths? Remember you have the choice of both glasses and contact lenses so if vanity is playing on your mind you really have no excuse not to at least consider contact lenses. Short session carp fishing is hard enough without the handicap of not being able to locate the fish in the first place!

These carp were feet from the margin but had I been less careful they would have spooked.

Glasses and contact lenses If you do need glasses
then get some. Any high street optician will be able to fix
you up with some clear ones, and many opticians now do
optically corrected sunglasses too. However the purpose of
sunglasses for a carp fisherman is not just to protect your
eyes but most importantly to be able to look into the water.
Are the glasses polarised? Because if not they are no real
aid to location. I use both Optilabs and Rapid Eyewear who
are specialist firms and make optically corrected glasses
aimed primarily at the fishing market. Not only are they
polarised but they are available in different colour lenses
as well. In bright sunlight a dark lens is ideal but from dusk
through to dawn an amber (yellow/brown) coloured lens
is superior. Yes, I did say dusk till dawn as I wear mine at
night too. Providing there is some light yellow or amber
lenses will really improve your night vision, thus allowing
you to watch for swirls or ripples.

These types of lenses are also ideal on dull days.
For those of you with perfect vision the same firms do
straightforward sunglasses as does the well-known Optix
company, too. You really have no excuses now not to be
able to observe with perfect vision.

Binoculars As an additional aid binoculars allow you to magnify your vision at range. When I am watching for bubblers I will often investigate the water with binoculars. These really allow you to pick up the type and size of bubbles that you would not be able to do with even the best of vision. When you are looking for coloured water at range they also help. On their own binoculars are very restrictive due to your reduced field of vision so spend time looking with your eyes but use the binoculars for pinpoint observation.

Extensive pads at Three Lakes but where exactly are the carp? By using binoculars I could see which pads were moving... game on!

Cap Again this sounds a little daft but when the sun is high a peaked cap or visor really cuts down on light creeping in above the glasses between your eyes and the inside of the lens. On a sunny day put your hand above your sunglasses and I bet you can see the difference already. No glare and improved vision. Always have a peaked cap with you and it will improve your observation techniques.

At range binoculars are invaluable to check out bubbles and movement.

Clothing Whilst bright tops are great for making your fish stand out for catch shots, when you are attempting to observe where the fish are this is a no-no. Wear dark or subtle clothing: with the explosion in the camouflage

market from hats to socks, clothing items can all be found in colours to match any background. The more muted the clothing is the less chance there is that you will scare the carp you wish to observe. And when time is at a premium the more time they are in front of you and not leaving the swim the better your odds of a take.

Footwear Carp are very attuned to vibration even on busy waters and although sound as such may not spook them I am convinced that vibration on the bank will not draw them into your swim and will put them on their guard. Ensure your footwear is practical but can be used in a way not to scare carp. I tend to use sports training shoes in muted colours unless it's the winter when I use boots with grip and warmth. Then it is down to you to tread carefully or face the consequences.

Leave the tackle in the car When it comes to locating carp walking round with a full barrow load of tackle is a way to rush your swim choice. If the car park is secure leave the tackle in the car: if not leave it with a friend who may already be fishing. By walking round with just a bucket in your hand, and suppressing the desire to pick the first swim you find fish in you can observe and locate carp a lot better.

Liquid If you are spending time looking for fish summer or winter it is important you do not become dehydrated. Take a bottle of water with you at all times. Your body is made up of around 70% water and the more dehydrated you are the more your concentration will suffer and the more likely you are to get a headache and rush your decision

Pen and paper If you see something significant write it down and leave nothing to chance. No matter how experienced you are and no matter how good you think your memory is nothing beats having a piece of paper to record your thoughts and sightings. When you walk and look for signs ensure it's with pen and paper. I tend to draw a quick sketch of the horizon and if possible any shadows and reflections on the water which will help me to record my sighting. Even if it only takes ten minutes to get back to the swim with your tackle if you didn't write it down your mind and memory can let you down.

Height The higher off the ground you are the better you will be able to look into the water. Ideally trees can be used to observe from but I can't stress too highly how dangerous this can be. Whilst this book does not come with a government health warning I will state now that this can be dangerous, frightening and can end with tragic consequences. Some anglers have ended up in wheelchairs or fared even worse through falling out of trees. Only climb them if it's allowed, safe and you are attired correctly. I am lucky in that I am able to climb quite easily but I will only go up wearing trainers, when it's not wet and when I am sure it's safe. No carp is worth risking your health and future.

You need to believe you will find them - the 'Mind Games' series I wrote in Carpworld from June 2009 to March 2010 is worth checking out if you want to see what motivation can do for all aspects of your carp fishing.

A sole pursuit Whilst it has been said that two pairs of eyes are better than one on your short sessions that is not so. You want to put all the balls in your court and a person on his own tends to be a lot quieter than a pair of anglers. You alone are responsible for getting in the right swim so try to do this on your own without being distracted by friends or other anglers.

Mindset The final part of observation really is mindset. If you walk around believing you are not going to find any carp you probably won't as you will end up rushing and not looking properly. In all likelihood you will simply choose a swim you 'fancy'. How is that for wasting your time on a short session? You need to have that positive mental attitude that I talk about. Keep saying to yourself that you will find them sooner or later. Negative attitudes breed negative results so snap out of that straightaway. I don't care that others may not have seen anything, you can and you will – believe it!

One of eight fish in a night - I found fish in an area that according to the books would be a waste of time. If I'd not been on my own I bet I wouldn't have even walked to the area.

Location

The best bit of advice I have ever read on location was when Tim Paisley was writing about locating

carp in the winter months. Although he too had read all the advice on 'location' his view quite simply was 'they are where they are', and that's where you fish for them. Ever since words have been written about carp fishing authors will have expressed their opinions about where to find carp and, most importantly, why you will find them there. Believe me for every reason someone says carp will be in a certain place you can find equally convincing arguments for them not being there! I doubt there is a reader of this book who doesn't have their own views on where to find carp but although a carp is a carp is a carp they don't play by the rules, I can assure you. When it comes to short session carping by all means don't forget those golden rules about fishing into a wind, looking for clouded water and all that but what is important to you is the information you have available to you the day you are fishing. What I am going to do is cover some bullet points that I have always – and I mean 'always' – found to be a major factor when it comes to my location of carp on shorter sessions. See which points apply to you and I am sure they will help you far more than the golden oldies we can all trot out.

Observe, Locate, Succeed

Night time Although I was going to say that the dawn period was the best time to locate carp, with more and more waters under pressure from carp anglers the best time to see and hear them can be during the hours of darkness. If the rules of the water allow you to, if you can turn up in the middle of the night do so. I first saw this done by a friend of mine Geoff Bradshaw in the early 90s when he fished a syndicate I ran. He had limited time available and it was usually at a weekend. He would turn up in the middle of the night, watch for fish whilst most of the anglers were asleep and come dawn he was set up, usually in places where nobody would have dreamt of fishing. On his short sessions he caught more than most. Fish can feel a lot more comfortable at night and will often show themselves quite freely.

Dawn Almost as good as the night time period and on less pressurised waters can be the best time to see them. But in the summer months that can mean the alarm clock going at 3.00a.m. and you looking whilst fighting back the desire for just ten more minutes in bed or on the bedchair. How much do you want to be on the fish? How little time do you have to fish effectively for them? Well surely a little lost sleep is not too much of a price to pay.

Dusk Particularly in the colder months carp and coarse fish are at their most active on the surface as the light starts to fade. Often I will not even decide on a swim until the dusk period, and once I have made a choice it will be the surface movements that will help me to decide where to cast my end tackle. Sitting in the bivvy watching a DVD or socialising with others may cost you dearly at this time so give the water your full attention.

The final part of observation and location is that the past was the past and today you have your chance to get it right. Make sure that your ability to observe is as good as you can make it: don't get bogged down with where they should be but concentrate on where they are.

Chapter Five
Make Swim Choice the Right Choice

nce you've researched the water as much as you can, and hopefully visited it at least once or twice to see how it appears in the flesh, then every future trip to it when you are fishing must be seen with an open mind, albeit in the knowledge you WILL build up each and every time you go. Whilst it is possible to succeed by fishing a variety of swims, when it comes to consistent short session success you really should try to focus all your attention on getting in the right swim each and every time you go. You won't always get what you think is the 'best' swim on the day, but the important thing is to use all your knowledge and commonsense to make the best choice of what is available to you as often as you can. When I talk about swim choice there are five main aspects I will look at, as follows: 'On the way to the water', 'Arriving at the water', 'Walking round the water', 'Making your decision' and 'Sticking with your decision'. All of these have one main consideration in that you must try to make the most of the time you have available even though at times that can be difficult.

On Your Way to the Water
If magazines and the like are to be believed it is wholly wrong to make your choice before you get to the water and no successful angler ever would dream of doing such a thing. Rubbish! Yes, rubbish! Let me tell you from my own experience and from talking to some of the best carp anglers in the country once you know a little bit about a water you are targeting you will inevitably have some initial thoughts as to swim choice as you get in the car and make your way there. The more you know a water the more your mind will have started piecing together the jigsaw puzzle we call carp location and inevitably it will be calculating where it thinks your best chances of

success are. This is the knowledge that you have over an angler who has never fished the water before, never visited the water before and in effect is 'fishing blind'. You would expect that if a warm wind is blowing you will find carp in the shallows, just as you'd expect the carp not to be in the shallows in the winter if that same wind, but colder, was blowing into it. The more you fish a water the more your memory and commonsense will give you some initial ideas about where you'd expect to find the carp.

I was never keen on this swim as everybody used to like to socialise in it, but if that's where the carp were then that's where I was.

However, what you do need to be aware of is falling into the trap of doing all the decision-making before you get there. You can only make an informed decision as to swim choice when you have as much information as possible each and every time you get there. That information will include what you know from past experiences, but it can only be complete when you take into consideration what the conditions are like on the day, where the other anglers are and most importantly what you see when you are there. Any decision made without all those considerations is not a complete one and may catch you out. So when you are driving to the water there is nothing wrong with thinking about where you'd expect them to be but you must not let that alone dictate swim choice.

Just one additional point on this aspect is that when I drive to the water I try and clear as much out of my mind so that the time in the car, be it ten minutes or three hours, is time concentrating solely on the fishing ahead. On short sessions you won't have the luxury of 'thinking yourself into a session' and every minute needs to be used wisely. I don't have music on, I certainly don't take calls and I turn my carp brain on as I call it. I know Lee Jackson does the same thing 'getting in the mode' as he calls it. Get rid of the day to day rubbish and concentrate solely on doing the best you can in the time you have.

Arriving at the Water

If your mind is in carp mode and it's been computing where you think the carp will be, pulling into the car park can make or break many an angler's confidence. The more cars there are the more some carp anglers' confidence will evaporate. In a sense that's okay especially on a water where you have anglers who know what they are doing fishing it. They probably have put in the legwork and if they are clever enough they will be in the swims that were the best choice when they arrived. However, a water is a living breathing thing and what may have been the right choice an hour ago could well be the wrong choice now. So don't let the negative vibes creep in... you haven't even started yet have you?

NO FISHING

My view nowadays is that it is a clean slate as I arrive and if a swim is taken it simply doesn't exist as a choice for me. So on a water with say 50 swims and five are already gone I have a water with 45 swims to make an informed choice from. Although this is an obvious point you need to remember that you are targeting carp which are trapped within that water, not birdlife which could have left the area anyway. Carp do not materialise here and there, they move from area to area in the lake, and whilst there may be some areas that 'seem to' produce more than others, unless you have a very low stocking density you have a good chance of being able to get on fish no matter how short the session is. Say the water is five to 10 acres and has say between a 100 and 200 fish, do you really think that they are all in five swims? Of course you don't. You are looking to catch a fish, or maybe two, and if conditions are right

and you get it right you may get a multiple catch. You can do that but not if you are de-motivated enough to think that five previously taken swims hold all the fish.

Yeah right! It may have been once but what matters is the day you or I are looking in it.

Walking Round the Water

Although I don't want to duplicate what I wrote in the previous chapter on observation and location this aspect really does get completely messed up at times even by the best intentioned of writers. We all go fishing for different reasons and I would imagine that my fishing is not too dissimilar to what many readers of this book do, or can do. You've had a hard day at work and all you really want to do is get set up and catch a carp or two, not spend hours walking and looking for carp that you may never even see. Well don't worry, that's not uncommon and for those

Before I make my final decision I will sometimes sit and wait, have one more drink to unwind and make a rational, not rushed, decision.

of us who have to fish shorter sessions and don't necessarily want to lose the fact that you need to enjoy it as well, at times it has to be a compromise. On smaller waters, yes, you can do a few circuits looking for fish but any swim choice will have to be a compromise. How many fish are there in it? If it's a small stocking level and you see one early on maybe that's the place to drop the bucket. However, if it's highly-stocked maybe you should look for a larger group of fish? What time do you have on the day? What are the weather conditions? Is it dusk? Is it feasible to cast out in the dark if it's a weedy water? All these are the realities of carp fishing which can at times be far removed from the advice given to

I was sure I was in the right swim but then the carp moved a little to my left and I had to move again.

keep looking until you find them. My advice is quite simple! If I have a good knowledge of the number of fish that are in the lake I will spend as much time as possible looking providing I do not unduly affect the time I can spend catching. If it's a day session I would be more inclined to keep looking until I found them. On an overnighter I will be limited due to decreasing light levels, setting up and fishing accurately and effectively.

Because short session carp fishing is about compromises you can only make that decision on the day. The more experienced you are the more you will know how much time to devote. If in doubt spend more time looking than fishing, especially on a bigger water. As you look remember what I said previously in that you should do it properly or not at all. You should be looking for the fish, not just looking to see if your favourite swim is taken or not! Your eyes should never leave the water and your carp brain should be fully on. More likely than not other anglers will be present and you really need to decide whether you ask them for help or not. The less I know about a water the more I will ask. The more I know the more I will use my judgement, but if I see nothing I may seek pointers from those present. Some anglers will say nothing, and some will perhaps give you too much information even. An opinion is an opinion but a wet mat is a whole different thing if you get my drift? Let their advice, or lack of it, be just a piece of the big picture when it comes to swim choice. I guess that most of you know what to look for so I am not going to cover all the things that you need to consider. Look for visual signs of carp and carp feeding, from bubbles to backs out of the water; it all helps when looking at that swim choice.

Making Your Decision
At some stage you are going to have to make a decision and although it won't be a final one it is the starting point to the time you have left. Modern day life can be rush, rush rush, and carp fishing is no different really.

I have made the mistake, and I guess I still do at times, of wanting to get cast out as soon as possible and will from time to time rush that most important of decisions. That's reality my friends and you and I won't be the first or the last to make such a mistake.

Let's say you've made the decision and barrowed the gear round, what next? Well the temptation is to get the rods out and get fishing, but that's not what I'd always advise you to do. Obviously if there are carp crashing out in front of you then get a bait to them if that won't spook them. However, if you've made an educated decision based on where you think they are don't be in a mad rush to get cast out. Take a few moments to catch your breath and reevaluate that decision. In summer I will get the

I set up in one swim but then moved as an angler to my left was stopping the fish moving through to me. The move was worth it and I had three in quick succession.

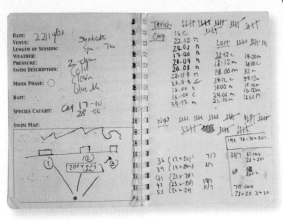

Every detail was written down and eventually a comprehensive plan was drawn up of the water.

water out and cool down for a moment, getting my head into gear. In winter unless they are dire conditions I will sit on the bucket and think. This is the choice I have made, is it the right one? Really? Do I think this now as I am sitting in the swim, or am I just in a rush to get set up and fishing? If you are honest with yourself you will know the answer to that! What affect will other anglers have on my fishing if they are nearby? Is this the best swim to fish bearing in mind where I am going to put the end tackles? Often the best swim is not necessarily the one with the fish out in front of you. Maybe a swim to the left or right would be better? What is the weed like for landing fish you hook? How much water can you command, and so on…

Most importantly of all, for the time you have left is this the right choice? Although carp may well be in front of you consider how much time you have. If it's an overnighter are the fish going to move out at night? If it's a day session how long do you think the carp will stay in this area, and so on? Where they are now is not necessarily where they may well be for the main part of your session. If it's a more difficult lake and you are literally lucky to get a bite then finding them can be enough. However if it's a more prolific lake you may want to look at the best swim to exploit a multiple catch. It's not as easy as some writers make it seem, is it?

Sticking With Your Decision

Once you've made the decision, and let's say got the rods out, you then need to decide whether to stick with the decision. On an overnighter you may not have much choice, although I have moved during a night session, but only when I have had the following day to fish as well. It's all well and good saying you should move at all times but you really need to balance that advice with still enjoying it. On a day session I will often not even take the tackle off the barrow so that I can move quickly if need be.

Make Swim Choice the Right Choice

However, if it's raining or snowing I may need the shelter up. If I haven't seen fish and the swim choice was an educated guess then I'd be more inclined to move if I saw fish. However, if I'd seen fish in front of me I'd have to see more elsewhere to move to them. Sometimes I will move if other anglers drop in close to me and spook my fish, or I think they will stop fish coming to me, but I will only move if I can come up with an informed choice as to what would be better. Moving for moving's sake is not an informed choice! At the end of the day whether you stay or go will always be down to you and your mental strength. If you have the belief to do it, the drive to complete it and the organisational skills to do it properly then it is no big deal. If any of those are missing it's a lot harder and you need to look at them and see how you can address the issues. Swim choice is not just about weedbeds and bubblers, it's mainly about you, your motivation, and your carp brain.

The perfect carp water? I chose this swim so I was not sitting on top of the margin patrolling fish to my left.

Chapter Six
Tackle: Do You Really Need it All?

This is not a book about taking up carp fishing or any one particular discipline of carp fishing, so I don't intend to rehash all the old favourites when I look at the items that contribute to success on short session fishing. I would hazard a guess that most of you have more than adequate fishing tackle and simply want advice on how to make the most of the short time you have to put it to best effect. What I am going to do is look at the major items and pass on some tips and thoughts that will contribute to getting the best from the product you've chosen. Tackle that works as it is intended to will not let you down and when time is at a premium you simply don't want to get it wrong.

Having been carp fishing over 25 years I have tried most items, or at least seen them used and abused on the bank. Time and success has meant that I have been able to equip myself with what I feel are the best items for me and my fishing. Now I am not for one second saying that you need to go out and buy a Daiwa Infinity rod and Basia reel or Nash Titan bivvy; that's not necessary at all, unless you can afford to. Your prime concern is to get a permit for the right water, to spend money getting to and from the lake and be able to buy the right bait and the best quality end tackle items to ensure that you hook and land the carp. Of course it's nice to have the 'best' gear if that's what people want to call it but be sure in your own mind that it is necessary. Like short session carp fishing spending money is always a compromise. If I buy this bivvy, rod, reel or whatever what effect will it have on my funds to go fishing? If you are simply building up a mountain of tackle but don't go, or can't afford to go often enough you are not going to succeed. Having seen top anglers catch all the fish they wanted using scruffy gear I can assure you that having the best possible gear is no substitute for time on the bank and effort. Right, I am sure you get the point I hope so let's look at the essential items.

Rods

Although it would be tempting to say any rod will do in all seriousness, in certain situations that just isn't so. One day you may be fishing at 10 yards and another day hurling a loaded PVA bag 70 yards accurately and your rod has to be able to cope with a number of situations. If it's working for you at the moment that's great but you really do get what you pay for. I find that with a rod around the 2¾lb test curve with a degree of backbone to it I can cast heavier leads, feeders and PVA bags longer distances more accurately. The backbone helps you to clamp down hard when you are fishing in weed and although there is always talk of pulling hooks out close in with strong rods that is often due to poor technique and fine wired hooks coupled with heavy leads. You must be able to be accurate to at least 80 yards and should be able to cast 100 yards. Most anglers tend to fish at 30 to 60 yards but often that is because they are uncomfortable, or not able to fish effectively at longer ranges. If you can't fish beyond

A top of the range Daiwa rod and reel combination meant I could whack a bait into position even into a strong head wind.

By marking my rod sleeves I can use the same clipped up rods to put the baits exactly in the same place when I am doing two nights in a row.

60 yards then you seriously need to look at the rods you are using. With the competition in the market companies are making the best a lot more readily available, and even the top of the range rods from Daiwa are affordable. Second-hand rods which have been looked after are a good bet, too, so check out the adverts in magazines or your local tackle shop. Whatever rod you do pick or use ensure it is kept clean and as well maintained as possible. Bent rings will cost you distance and cause crack offs as the line wraps round them. The cleaner the rod is any line slap on the cast will have negligible effect on the distance you cast and when you are playing fish your hands are not going to slip due to caked-on mud and bait greasing the handle.

Reels

There is a similar situation with reels. The two prime considerations are that it allows you to cast to the spots you want to and land the fish you are hooking. Large spooled reels are commonplace now but unless you are spending serious amounts of money on a reel like the Daiwa Basia there will be a compromise between size and weight. The bigger the reel gets the heavier it gets, which means it will not be as easy to cast with accurately due to its weight. Look at the reels you are using and if you can load them with say 15lb main line and cast around 80 yards accurately and consistently then size-wise they are ideal.

I do use the best I can but the basic pit reels will suffice if money is tight.

If not you really should be looking at a reel with a larger spool. The bigger the spool the better heavier line flies off on the cast – when loaded correctly – and the more accurate you will be.

Size alone is not the only consideration as it's important that the drag or clutch is smooth and consistent for playing fish. Whilst some anglers still backwind to play fish as you become more experienced you should use the clutch on the reel and the rod as an extension of your arm to lead the carp in like a dog on a lead. Better quality reels like the Daiwa range and Shimano range have silky smooth drags which don't jerk. As with rods a reel is only as good as its maintenance. In fact, reels tolerate less abuse than rods so keep them clean and well maintained. If your reel is not as good as the day you got it then get it serviced.

Because I like to fish my rods as low as possible inevitably my reels are only an inch or two from the ground. To reduce grit and mud getting into them particularly when it rains I have a cut down piece of rubber car mat under each reel about 8" square, a simple little idea that prolongs the life of the reel and saves you money for more important things. Whatever reel you use ensure you have spare spools for it. On short sessions you must use the right gear and if one day it would be best to use a fluorocarbon main line and another day a heavy-duty monofilament then having spare spools loaded up ready make it a lot easier. No one main line will cover all situations so a set of spare spools is a must.

Top **If you use fluorocarbon then soften it first in warm water, it will load and cast beautifully.**

Whatever line you get follow the instructions, load it properly and get the best from it.

Main Line

When I cover the specifics of spring, summer and winter fishing I will look at the best lines to go for so I intend to keep it brief in this chapter. No one line will cover all situations and in my opinion a compromise is unnecessary when you should have spare spools loaded with alternatives. For most anglers you should use fluorocarbon and monofilament main lines most of the time with braid on your marker rod. Fluorocarbon like X-line sinks well so in clear, shallow waters it is ideal as it is less obvious to the carp. However, these lines are a lot more expensive and do not cast as well, nor are they particularly user-friendly unless you are an experienced angler. In most other situations I would look to a monofilament line like Daiwa Sensor or Nash Bullet XT. These are a lot cheaper

so you can change them more often, they have better abrasion resistance for fishing in weed, cast a lot better and are a lot more user-friendly.

Whatever line you choose it will only be as good as the angler loading and using it. Look at the instructions that come with the line and follow them when you load the reel. If you load them incorrectly line twist will build up which will reduce distance and strength and will cost you fish. Whatever line I use I always soak and load it in warm water to soften it. Simply place the spool in a bowl of warm water for 10 minutes and then load it as per the instructions with the line still in the warm water. It loads a lot easier and smoother this way and will cast further and behave

Some say I have OCD. I like to think I am prepared for all eventualities. Tidy tackle stack means I know when to restock.

better. Whatever line you use always inspect it as you use it and if there are any signs of damage then change it. The cost is immaterial compared to the money you spend on other items of tackle so if in doubt re-spool. This can be more expensive with fluorocarbon but on short sessions you simply cannot skimp on anything that will improve your chances of success.

Buzzers

For me buzzers need just two main qualities, especially on my short sessions. They need to be reliable enough so that come sun, rain or ice they don't pack up and they need to be sensitive enough to indicate audibly a take from a carp that does not necessarily bolt off and give me a 'one-toner'.

Ten years old and still going strong - my Fox buzzers.

Again you get what you pay for and the more you spend the more 'bolt-ons' you will end up getting. The buzzers I use now I have had for nearly 10 years and other than one service from Fox they are still going strong. Although mine have all the adjustments that you could ever need other than volume I hardly ever mess with the settings. What I do like is a remote that means I can turn my buzzers down low to avoid annoying everybody around me, and in winter if I have to sit inside the shelter I can still here the single bleep that tells me a carp may be hooked.

A couple of little tips I would give you is that although blue is a bright colour for an LED and remote it can blind you at night and can be very difficult to pick up in bright sunlight. Secondly when you set your buzzers up unless your rods are parallel to the ground you sometimes do not always get the best registration. I tend to raise the tips slightly which improves the pressure of the line on the wheel/vibro and improves registration.

Finally buzzers are only as good as your care of them so dry them as often as possible, replace the batteries as and when needed and don't use anything other than a Duracell battery. On a short session it's vital to not miss anything so don't cut corners. At the end of the session they go back in the carry case which allows me to leave the heads screwed onto a cut down inner stick from the Nash Grippa Stix range. When it comes to setting up next time I simply pop them into whatever length of front stick I want so saving a lot of time. The only other buzzers I have are a very old pair of Stevie Neville roller ones which were marketed by Nash. The pair of these sit in my stalking holdall so if I do decide to stalk and want to rest my eyes for a minute I can stick the rods on them.

Solar Line Clip.
I would not be without them to improve bite registration.

Visual Indicators

With so many to chose from it really does boil down to personal choice. They need to be heavy enough to show a drop back at range and constructed in a way that they don't snag your line when slack lining. Although I have used a lot of visual indicators the tackle bag now simply has a set of Nash SlapHeads in them. Because all the components are interchangeable I can simply swap heads (they weigh from 4 grams to 18 grams) depending on how far out I am fishing and the registration I am looking for. Sometimes I have three different weight SlapHeads on because I am fishing three rods at different ranges: now when did you last see that? Look after whatever visual indicator you chose and remember what it's there for. If you are using fluorocarbon at range then you will need to use a heavy visual indicator to amplify the movement. However, when slack-lining at close range the lightest possible bobbin will suffice as a heavy bobbin will tighten your line. I always use the Solar line clips on my rods so that I can create a deep 'V' between clip and bobbin and buzzer. This accentuates movement to both your eye and to the buzzer which indicates the take. By moving the clip up and down the rod you can fine tune it for maximum effect. Because I tend to fish my rods quite low, to keep the SlapHeads out of the bankside vegetation, again I have some cut down rubber car mats, not only does this keep the grass and mud off the bobbins but it also allows me to see them more easily.

Bank Sticks
I have long been a fan of single bank sticks providing the terrain you are fishing on allows you to push them into it. By using a single bank stick front and rear I can point my rod directly at the end tackle, so improving bite indication and lessening the chances of the rod been dragged off the rest by a carp that kites left or right instantly. The bank sticks are the Nash Bank Stix ones which I have a variety of in my holdall. This means I can fish my rod tips high or low as needed by simply swapping the outer sticks around. That way I am dictating the set up rather than letting my lack of preparation dictate how I have to fish. Inside my stalking bag I have a pair of Gardner Stalking Sticks which are very light, very small and ideal for pushing into any terrain when creeping round and sitting well back.
I also have in the car a Fox Euro Pod just in case the venue has swims that I can't push my bank sticks into. I once drove all the way down to Catch 22 in Norfolk without a rod pod only to find that the swims I wanted to be in were on staging... Ahhhhh! Don't let the swim dictate to you, you dictate to the swim how you want to fish your rods for maximum effect.

Landing Nets
As long as they, yes THEY, are big enough and strong enough game over. I always take two nets with me so

that when I land a carp I can leave it in the net, unclip my hook length and get the rod back out into position as I detail fully in the multiple catches chapter. Having a landing net each side of the swim makes it far easier to land fish at night and with one in the net I have sometimes had one on the recast. Look after them, dry them after each trip and, most importantly, fill them!

Basic I know, but I was there to catch not pose... and I did.

Shelter

Because we are looking at the best approaches to short session carp fishing shelters don't feature high on my list of 'vitals'. However, unless I am walking round the pond in summer with my stalking gear I will always take some form of shelter with me. If conditions at the lake change and I have to go home because of the weather then I am costing myself time. A light brolly in the holdall will mean I don't waste that valuable time. For overnighters I choose something a little more substantial like a Nash Oval Plus with the extended sides which protect the bedchair. I always use a cut down groundsheet which takes about 20 seconds to put down and weighs very little. No point in skimping when there is no need to. I never have a front on the shelter as I want to be able to see the water at all times even when lying on my bedchair. Pegs are always quality

Looks a lot? Well it all goes on the Nash Trax barrow for an overnighter.

screw in ones and each year I treat the shelter to a reseal with the fabric spray you can get from any camping store like Millets or Blacks. Whilst I'm not unduly worried about condensation on a short session I know that one treatment each year makes the shelter much more waterproof, especially round the seems. A dry short session angler is a more focussed short session angler.

Bedchair and Seat

Again you pay your money and get what you pay for. Mine is the brilliant Daiwa Infinity bedchair which I take on overnighters. For day sessions I take a small low chair in winter but in the summer I take a Nash Bucket Cushion. Providing I can get it on the barrow a bedchair is not high on my list of essentials. That said you need to enjoy your fishing and be comfortable, especially on overnighters. If you are aching when you leave you will find an excuse not to do a second night!

Luggage

As I tend to barrow my gear everywhere the luggage I use takes all my gear and is easy to load. Two barrow bags take all the tackle that does not go in the rod bag. The rods each go in single sleeves in the rod bag. The bedchair and

Tackle: Do you Really Need it All?

stuff goes in the bedchair bag. Other than the bait in the
freezer bag, if it doesn't fit into either of the four mentioned
bags it isn't coming with me. When you see it in the flesh
it looks a lot but as long as it does not stop me pushing the
barrow then it comes along.

Barrow
Unless I am walking round stalking or floater fishing, or if
the terrain does not make it possible, I will always barrow
my gear around. The one I use is a Nash Trax Terrain which
fits easily in the back of the Jeep, and one pin secures
the lot. On short sessions I could not be bothered piecing
together some of the barrows I see on sale. Freezer bag
in the bag under the barrow, two barrow bags on top, the
bedchair bag on top of that and finally the rod holdall
with up to five rods on top of that. One bungee strap
secures all and away we go to the best swim for our
short session success.

One of eight carp in a
night. The tackle did
the trick but it is only
part of the equation.

Chapter Seven
Let's Get Riggy!

I n a book aimed purely and simply at catching carp on short sessions some subjects won't get the attention to detail that perhaps some readers think they deserve. Whilst in part this may be true, in another way it is important that you see that no one subject dominates the book. Being successful on short sessions is not just down to any one aspect, it's down to them all. If you do over-emphasise one aspect of your fishing to the detriment of others you will not be as successful as you should be. Of all the areas I think anglers get confused about, or off course, it's carp rigs. Time and time again I see anglers turn up and talk to me not about where I think the carp are, not about how the weather may influence swim choice and so on but about how they have read about a new rig and it's going to make all the difference. It's almost as though the effort and singular thought process goes into the tying of the rig rather than finding the carp. Been there, tied it up and blanked.

End tackles and presentations are important but no more so than any of the other information you find in this book. What I am about to detail are safe and effective rigs which will catch carp on any water, and even when you do need to adapt them they are sound starting points for any successful short-session angler. The rig bits I detail are what I use and know work but if the ones you want to use provide the same rig mechanics that's fine too. All items are a matter of preference and, as I am renowned for saying, 'If it ain't bust don't fix it...'

End Tackles
Five in all, and all end tackles I use on a variety of waters, have done for years and no doubt will continue to do so. None of them started out as you see them in the diagrams today but are down to years of experimenting, fine-tuning

and hundreds of carp
caught from far and wide.
I've included some tips and
advice on each one but
there are a few pointers I
will give in advance which
apply to any that you use or
are considering.

End Tackle Storage

Most anglers I see fishing,
myself included, have the
end tackle already tied up
and on the rod when they

It's not just the rig that
matters but where you
cast it. Midwinter on a
prolific venue and I'm
waiting for a carp to
show itself so I can put
a stringer to it.

arrive. That's fine, but when you select your swim the end
tackle you use should be the one best suited to the swim,
not just what happens to be on the rod. With leaders and
leadcore setups that's fine as all you need to do is carefully
snip off the rig without damaging the loop on the leader
and tie on the right rig. However, if leaders are banned and
you are using tubing it may take a little longer, but do it.
The minute or two to tie it up is not wasted so don't be lazy.

To store my end tackles I construct as many variants
as I feel might be needed, without a lead of course. I then
place them in small plastic sleeves, like the ones hooks and
rig bits come in, then store them in my tackle box. This is
time saving and very efficient for short sessions.

Lead Size

The first obvious point is that it needs to be heavy enough
to reach the spot you are casting to and, in my opinion,
usually no more. Very heavy leads are harder to feel down
properly, make a lot of noise on entry and at times are
unnecessary. My usual size as you will see is one and a half
to two and a half ounces. It's not just the lead that sets the
hook, it's the sharpness of the hook, drag of the end tackle
and so on. Lighter is best for most fishing.

Tubing, Leadcore or Leader?

Most of my setups include the Nash Diffusion Quick Sink
Limpet Leaders as they blend in with any lakebed and
are very reliable. Occasionally I will use leadcore when I
am Chod fishing and want the weight of the leadcore to
pull the hook in. Some waters ban leaders of any kind in

From 1oz to 4oz and in all designs just in case.

which case I use the Nash Diffusion No Spook tubing or ESP Anchor Rig tubing with equal confidence. Providing the product blends in, is safe and does not affect the mechanics of the end tackle it's fine.

Camouflage Effect

With the great products that Nash, Gardner and Korda have in their range you really can blend in to match most lakebeds. Is it necessary? Well personally I think it is, and it won't cost you any fish by making it as unobvious as possible, will it? I am sure carp always know they are being fished for and by using end tackle that blends in you are reducing, but not completely negating, the spook factor.

Safety

Whatever end tackle you use it must be safe and in the event of a crack-off or snagged-up fish the carp must be able to discharge the lead. No rig is 100% safe but all we can do is our best. The more inexperienced you are the better it is to copy exactly from the product information you find with each product, and not to mix different product ranges.

Korda Safe Zone Leader

Half-inch loop of 4lb mono

Tied On Lead End Tackle

At close range in weed this is ideal as your chances of landing a carp safely are hugely improved once the lead is dumped. For stalking you can lower the lead down but for anything beyond that simply PVA the lead to a Safe Zone Leader or fish it in a PVA bag. The loop must be at least half an inch long so that it can bump off easily when playing the fish in the weed, hence the dumpy lead which improves this effect.

Korda Swivel
Square lead 1-2oz
(swivel removed)

Lead clip and matching tail rubber

Nash Diffusion Camo Leader

Lead Clip End Tackle

For most situations where there is weed this is ideal, but in heavier weed it's the tied on end tackle that is best. Most companies sell the lead clip and I personally rate the Nash and ESP ones highly. Don't push the tail rubber on too hard if you want the lead to discharge and, if possible, don't mix clip and rubbers from different companies as they are designed only for their own range. For many of you fishing waters with limited weed this clip will be a great starting point for an end tackle.

Korda Swivel
Square lead 1-3oz

Korda In-line Square Lead 1½ – 3½oz

Nash Diffusion Camo Leader

In-Line End Tackle

When the bottom is clear of weed, say on a sandy bottom or gravel, I prefer this in-line version to a lead clip. The impact of the lead weight is felt quicker and they do fly further and more accurately when casting.

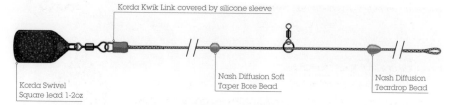

Korda Kwik Link covered by silicone sleeve

Nash Diffusion Soft Taper Bore Bead

Nash Diffusion Teardrop Bead

Korda Swivel Square lead 1-2oz

Running Chod End Tackle

The Chod Rig really does seem to have exploded in popularity in recent years and when used in the right circumstances it's a great and effective end tackle. If you set the beads correctly you can be pretty sure that the hookbait will be visible to the carp and not snarled up in weed. In light weed I use the ready-tied Kryston Score leadcore leaders, but in heavier weed I go for the Nash Diffusion Quick Sink Limpet leaders because I am uncomfortable using leadcore in weed for safety reasons. It can loop around weed and kink which can make it unsafe.

The key to Chod end tackles, in my opinion, is using as light a lead as possible to hit the mark. It is not the lead that's pricking the hook in but the carp levelling up against the leader and panicking, so pulling the hook home. Because the Chod presentation runs between the beads it cannot lever or bounce the hook out against the lead. I like to have a gap of around 12 inches for the Micro Rig Ring Swivel to move on so that the hookbait is always visible to the carp. The lead is fished on a clip so I can pick the lightest one possible: a heavy one will often pop the hook out of the carp's mouth when playing it as the Chod hooklink runs down to the lead.

Size 8 Ring Swivel

Nash Diffusion Camo Leader

Korda Skyliner Lead 1½-3oz

Mag-Aligner End Tackle

For short-range maggot fishing I use the safety clip or in-line end tackle, but for 30 yards or more I prefer this one. The Big Ring swivel allows you to loop on your stocking of maggots and then nick home the hookpoint so making it tangle-proof. Use the lightest lead possible to hit the distance as a heavy lead and small hooks that work best with the Mag-Aligner can result in hookpulls.

Presentations

Just as with end tackles the presentations I have detailed have come through years of fine-tuning and are my starting point for all my short session fishing. They will certainly catch on most waters that you target but whichever one you choose to add to the appropriate end tackle there are some considerations to bear in mind.

A variety of hooklengths to cover all the situations I find myself in.

Knots

Not all knots work with different materials, so despite the ones I detail within this book, if you are not using the same rig bits as me I cannot promise you the same efficiency. Ensure you research and find the correct knot for the material you are knotting. I always test my hook knot by holding the hookshank with forceps and use a straight angle of pull. For loops I have a number of pieces of dowelling that range from half to two inches in diameter so I can form and bed in the Loop Knot correctly

Rig Glue

Although I use rig glue on some rigs not all materials respond to it and some materials will weaken from its use. I use the minimum possible and use it only to prevent slippage in an effort to make good a bad knot.

Length of the Presentation

Normally I look at around 6-8 inches but will tend to go
shorter in weed and longer in clearer water situations. If
you are not getting takes and everything else is fine it may
be that you are simply duplicating what everyone else is
doing and may need to change. However, if everything
else is right you will catch so don't get sidetracked into
thinking that a longer hooklength is more important than
moving to a showing fish!

Steaming

If I use a coated braid, stiff link or fluorocarbon that I
have tied at home I steam the product for rigidity. I have
never found it to weaken the material and because I do it
carefully at home nor should it. Doing it on the bank may
weaken it, but that's not the steaming but the steamer!
Steaming straightens out your hooklength beautifully which
decreases tangles, pushes the hookbait away from the lead
and so on. Once tied up and stored the effect is fantastic, I
assure you.

Pinning Down

Because of the way carp feed the last thing I want is my
hooklength fouling their pecs if it loops up from the bottom.
A steamed hooklength will probably lie flat anyway, but
when using braid I smear it with Kryston Drop Em, or mud
from the lake bank to nail it down. Don't overdo it or you
will create too much rigidity in a product that is supposed
to be supple to perform correctly. The brilliant new Korda
Sinkers are ideal to use on hooklengths to nail them down
out of harm's way.

Camouflage

Just like end tackles the less obvious a presentation is the
better. Many products blend in anyway but using the
excellent TFG Disguise Colour-It pens you can colour your
products to match the area you are fishing. A dabbing
effect really breaks up continuous colours to make them
less blatant.

Hairs

Virtually all my Hairs are made using the Nash Bait Floss.
With pop-ups I loop them on and with bottom baits I use
a pierced bait on a standard Hair. Generally, I like at

least quarter to half inch between the top of the hookbait and bottom of the hookshank when fishing bottom baits to allow separation of the two and increased hooking efficiency. With pop-ups I tend to fish them on mini rings anyway so that the pop-up can move up and down the loop smoothly.

Crimps

When I am using ESP Stiff Bristle Filament in 20 or 25lb b.s. and want to form a loop crimps are always my first choice. Use them correctly and they are as strong as any knot and allow you to form the neatest of loops, small and large. The crimps are the Wychwood version and the pliers are from Fox. You must not use crimps on anything else other than the product I have named, please.

Something for every occasion - each item is the best I can get for my fishing.

Tangles

No rig is entirely tangle-proof but once you include a PVA bag it is less likely. When fishing single baits I always add some water-soluble foam that I squeeze over the hook and Hair. It stops tangles 100% and once the foam pops up vertically above where my end tackle is I will know its precise placement.

Quick Change Clips

There seems an absolute obsession in using these on all presentations... why? If you are using a PVA stick and need to draw the hooklink through it, fine. If you are catching plenty of fish and need to change rigs super-quick, fine, but otherwise... Personally, for most of you reading this it's just another unnecessary bit on the rig so stick to knotting your hooklength to the swivel, or looping it. Unless you really are speed fishing once you've landed your fish snip off the presentation and use a new one. Don't do something unless there is a good reason.

Bottom Bait Presentation

Simple and effective: I tend to use a coated braid but when fishing it in a PVA bag I will use braid straight through, such as Kryston Super Nova or Nash Ultrasilk. Usually the bait is a single cubed bottom bait but you can also use the setup for double bottom baits or Snowman presentations. Ideal to be fished on the lead clip, in-line or tied on lead end tackle.

Enterprise Corn Stop

Rig Ring

Gardner Mugga

Bottom bait

Silicone

1" of coating removed

Korda Sinker or tungsten rig putty

20lb E-S-P Strip-Teaze

Overhand loop knot

Fluorocarbon Presentation

In clearer conditions, particularly in spring and winter, I always use fluorocarbon as a hooklength. It tends to be less obvious in clear water conditions where everything can stand out. Because I want to use a flexible Hair with it I tie the Hair to the hook first and then the fluorocarbon over that pre-tied Hair. This is ideal with the in-line end tackle.

Enterprise Corn Stop

Bottom bait

Supple Hair

Gardner Longshank Incizor

Korda sinker or tungsten rig putty

Kryston Incognito Fluorocarbon hooklength

Overhand loop knot

Pop-Up, tied on with bait floss

Gardner Mugga

Quarter-inch coating removed

Rig Ring

Overhand loop knot

Tungsten Putty counterweight

20lb E-S-P Strip Tease

Overhand loop knot

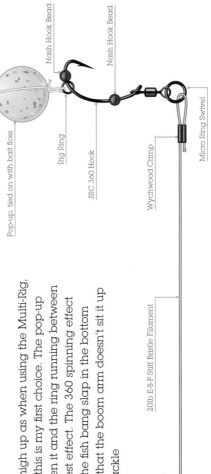

Pop-up, tied on with bait floss

Nash Hook Bead

Nash Hook Bead

Rig Ring

JRC 360 Hook

Wychwood Crimp

Micro Ring Swivel

20lb E-S-P Stiff Bristle Filament

Wychwood Crimp

Multi-Rig Presentation

For my bog-standard pop-up presentation this is my starting point. The break in the coating between counterweight and knot allows it to spin at 360 degrees which is so important. Sometimes I will overweight it if fishing a single bait but over a scattering of boilies I will critically-balance the presentation. Ideal to fish on the safety clip end tackle or tied on lead end tackle.

360 Rig Presentation

When I want to fish a pop-up, but not as high up as when using the Multi-Rig, on a clearer bottom then I'd use a Chod, this is my first choice. The pop-up needs to have a quarter-inch gap between it and the ring running between the beads on the shank of the hook for best effect. The 360 spinning effect is so effective and tends to always hook the fish bang slap in the bottom lip. This is best fished on clear bottoms so that the boom arm doesn't sit it up unnaturally. I use it with the in-line end tackle

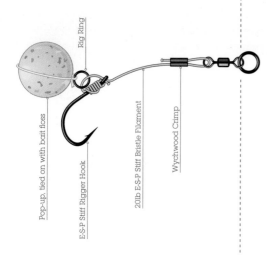

Pop-up, tied on with bait floss

Rig Ring

E-S-P Stiff Rigger Hook

20lb E-S-P Stiff Bristle Filament

Wychwood Crimp

Chod Presentation

Fished in conjunction with the Running Chod end tackle this is ideal for
fishing into anything other than solid weed. Because it can run between the
beads it will sit on, not in, the weed. I tend to fish this presentation a little
lower than most so that even without a curve in the Stiff Bristle Filament the
hookbait is no more than two inches from the leader. Best fished as a roving
single bait presentation into or over weed.

Mag-Aligner Presentation

When the small fish are not making it impossible – and particularly in the
winter and early spring – maggots are a very effective carp bait. I will go
down to a size 12 hook with two maggots on it but for the larger fish I find a
size 10 and three or four maggots is more effective. Although you can fish this
at shorter range inside a PVA bag full of maggots using an in-line or lead clip
end tackle, for fishing at thirty yards or more use the Mag-Aligner
end tackle.

Enterprise Imitation Maggots

Gardner Mugga

Enterprise Imitation Maggot

Coating removed

Korda Sinker or tungsten rig putty

15lb E-S-P Strip Tease

Overhand loop knot

Storage

If you are using a hooklink of less than 12 inch then the Korda Rig Safe is excellent and I have many with me at all times. However, don't let the length of the rig box dictate the length of your presentation! I am lucky in that I have had made for me a 24-inch rig box so that I can fish presentations that long when necessary. For braided presentations you can store them in rig wallets but if you are fishing a water which demands a long hook length then you will have to tie it up on the bank. The more you fish a water the more you will know what your likely starting points are going to be so there's nothing wrong with having some presentations tied in advance. However, don't end up using presentations because those are the ones you have with you rather than the ones you should be using.

So there you have a very straightforward look at carp rigs for the short session carp angler, but please remember that rigs are just part of the equation – no matter what your mind will try to tell you otherwise at times!

Mid-double common where I'd got the rods on leadcore end tackles but when I moved swims I changed to Diffusion leaders to avoid looping the leadcore over the weed in the new swim.

Chapter Eight
On The Money

Remember what I said at the start of the book that short session success is all about playing the percentage game? The more you get right the quicker success will come and with preparation and a little good fortune success will continue to come. Later in the book when I look at the seasons and the stalking and floater fishing disciplines I will look at the spots to fish to, but for the moment let's just imagine you have chosen the perfect water, the right swim and you are there with the tackle on the barrow. Obviously your carp brain will be in full flow and I hope that all your other thoughts will have been put to one side and you will have made an initial decision as to where to cast your baits.

Sounds like a normal session to you? Great it is! The only difference now is that no matter where you place your baits you should be able to put them in exactly the same spot again if you need to. When you cast out no matter how good or bad you feel your chances are you can never know whether the spot you cast your rod to will produce a run or not. That is the beauty of carp fishing. I have been in summer in perfect conditions and felt 100% confident of a take – and blanked. Yet in winter I have been sitting there at the end of my tether giving it my best shot but not expecting anything really, and off it's roared. Can you imagine getting a take and not being able to put it back to the same spot again? Be pretty stupid wouldn't it? Now I am not saying that you will always get another take from that spot but years of experience have taught me that more often than not, if I am going to get another take, especially on a short session, it will be from that spot. Although carp may well feed all over the water in front of you there will be places they prefer to feed, and there seems to be spots where for some reason or another they

are prepared to make a mistake with the hookbait. Find it, mark it and if it's a good one, exploit it. So the moral of the story is, summer or winter, full of confidence or having a crisis in confidence, you need to be in a position to put it back on the same spot, and the only way to do this is by preparation and accuracy.

The spot was almost 100 yards out but a combination of a sight line and tape meant I kept dropping it on the money each time as this hard-fighting fish proves.

Preparation

As soon as I am in the swim, providing I don't need to get a bait on a showing fish, the first thing out will be my notebook and pen. If I have been in the swim before no doubt there will already be a sketch of the swim with as many details as I thought useful. Forget the tiny little books you can get for fishing get one that is A4 size and large enough for you to include all the details you need. Draw a rough sketch of the swim and, when applicable, the far tree line. Whilst some lakes will be barren they are few and far between so a tree line is a must. I also draw the water's edge in front of the tree line so I can see swims, holes in trees etc. in relation to the tree line above them. If the water in front of you has islands or any other visual features between you and the far bank draw those too. And of course, if you do happen to see a fish roll whilst you are sketching then mark that down too.

Once the rods come out you need to decide where to position them taking into account what you saw on your walk round the water, or at least through hunches created by hard work carried out earlier. As I tend to fish my rods on single bank sticks it's a case of making sure that the rods are pointed at the spots I intend to fish to when I first put my baits out. Unless I am casting at a rolling fish where one cast is enough, I usually have two or three casts with a bare end tackle just to feel the nature of the lakebed. The hook lengths will stay in the rig box and I am simply casting the lead a couple of times so I know what's on the bottom. Once I have satisfied myself that the lakebed is one I can present my end tackle on I will do what I call a 'clipping cast'. This entails casting out the lead, and with my finger holding the line against the spool, feeling that lead down. If the lead hits the bottom as I want it to I will pay out around 3 inches of line and then put the line into the clip on the spool.

Top of the range Daiwa Basia and state of the art line clip for hitting the spot.

Plain old electricians' tape but make sure the line you fold it over is dry.

Line Clips on Your Spool

The purpose of the line clip in this case is to stop any more line being taken and to draw the lead back down to the same place. Obviously it is only for the cast and once the lead is in position the line is unclipped. To be fair most spool clips are good nowadays and from personal experience the ones on the modern day Daiwa reels are excellent. If they are too tight you will never be able to push your line behind the clip and if you did it may damage it. To cut out any worry over this I pull a piece of 30lb Power Gum into the clip and neatly trim it off around the clip. This raises the clip's height slightly making it easier to work with, and is kinder on your main line.

Once the line is in the clip wind in again and recast to the same spot which, until you become more experienced can take a bit of getting used too. Too hard a cast and the lead will snatch back and too soft a cast and you won't reach the clip. Either way it won't be on the spot. In time you will get used to it and I find that slightly leaning forward just as the lead is about to hit the water means I don't 'clonk' the clip but the leads arcs beautifully down. If the lead has hit the same spot you know the line is clipped up correctly. Next you need to mark the line so that you can know where to clip up each and every time.

Electrical Tape

If I am not fishing a prolific water where a take or a few takes is the absolute most I could expect then I use electrical tape. About three inches in front of where the line is clipped up I fold a piece of tape over the line - make sure the line is dry. Carefully trim the tape so it looks like a thin tube. I also mark the line with a TFG marker pen so that I can see in an instant if the tape has moved. When I use a fluorocarbon main line I mark it with black pen and when I use a darker monofilament I use white Tippex.

Power Gum

If the water I am on is more prolific and I am expecting a number of takes I will use a power gum stop knot. Although these are a little more bulky they do not tend to slip at all so are ideal for the more prolific waters. Again 3 inches in front of the clip tie that power gum stop knot, but in this case don't trim the tag ends too short. I tend to leave them about half an inch each side so they cast easier than stubs, which tend to 'jar' or jam on the cast.

If you push a piece of power gum under any line clip it will soften it and improve the life of your main line.

Now your line is clipped up get your sketch plan and mark on it the sight line you were casting towards. This could be a tree, telegraph pole or anything. Obviously as it gets darker many things will disappear so the top of a tree is a lot easier to cast to. With the line marked unclip your line, and by hand wind in a bit so that the tape or power gum is at the back of the spool, flick the bale arm over and wind in fully.

Now that your line is marked you know that providing you cast at the same sight line when you stand in the same place once in the clip it will keep dropping on the same spot. To find the clipping up point all I do is

One of the many that night in the dark. If I hadn't drawn my sight lines and also marked my main line, I certainly would not have caught as many.

cast past the spot and wind in till the tape or Power Gum appears. Once it is the same 3 inches from the clip I clip the line up and wind in fully. Tie on a hooklength and out it goes on the spot on each and every time. You must always remember to unclip once the lead thumps down or you may find your rod disappearing in the take, or the line breaking at the clip!

Sometimes when I am using a very fine main line I will actually place the tape in the line clip. This protects the line as the line going in the clip has a cushion of electrical tape around it.

Creeping up

Sometimes the spot you want to hit will be tight to a bush, weedbed, island or something solid! You then won't have the luxury of being able to overcast and draw back as 'too far' will see you landing in trouble rather than something wet! In such cases I 'creep up' on the spot by purposely dropping short and guessing how far short I am, pay out some line and clip up. I then wind in and recast: usually it drops a little short again so I repeat the process by unclipping and paying off a little more line, and so on. As you become more experienced you will be able to do this in two or three casts maximum. Yes I know it sounds a lot of effort but it has taken me a lot longer to write it than to ever do it! To me it's second nature and I can tell you from watching anglers on a whole variety of waters less than 25% ever do it. Near enough is their excuse: "Rubbish!" is my reply. Remember on short sessions you want as many things right as possible and casting clipped up is more than possible with some practice.

   If you decide not to continue with that marked spot take off the tape, draw a new sight line and clip up where you want it to drop. When I cover the red letter days in a later chapter you will see how important this process is to maximise your chances. If you are wondering about how to be accurate after dark, this too is covered later in the book.

   I can't stress how important being accurate is to the short session carper. Remember, you do not have the time to let them come to you and if you find that spot you really have to be able to get maximum results from minimum time.

They drained the lake and I took some pictures for my records. Look at the drop off on that bar. At times, a miss is as good as a mile.

Chapter Nine
Bait Delivery: Tools and Approach

lthough I am going to cover bait application in the specific chapters on seasons and those on floater fishing and stalking, I will say at the start of this chapter that when it comes to short session success many anglers spoil their chances by using too much bait, and what bait they do apply seems to go all over the place. Remember this book is all about success on short session carp fishing and not necessarily about applying a bait for long-term success, dominating a water with a bait and so on. It is about getting bites and fish on the bank in the limited angling time that you have.

Before we even start to look at how to deliver or apply bait you need to ask yourself one simple question. What is the purpose of any feed I am putting in that is not attached to my hook? Ever thought of that? No, for a long time I didn't either. One of the most important things I have taught myself to do is to only do something when I can logically explain to myself why I am doing it. That I get it wrong does not matter so much, the important factor is that I have a reason for what I am doing. Now I know why I attach a bait to my hook… that is because I want the carp to sample it and hopefully hook itself, or give me an indication which allows me to strike that hook home. However, when it comes to additional feed why am I applying it? Because that's what everybody else is doing at the water? Because that's what I always do? Because of what I've seen in the magazines and on film? Marker rod, hookbait and spod or catapult a pile of feed? Why? On short sessions, even on prolific waters, your first aim is to get a take and land the fish. Occasionally you will have your red letter day but if you have limited time and always bait up for a multiple catch I will bet that you will fail more than you succeed. For the longer-stay angler too much feed but plenty of time will probably mean that sooner or later a carp will make a mistake with your hookbait and you will catch one. Imagine if you got it right earlier and didn't have to wait all that time?

Now this does not just apply to boilies; I have seen over-baiting on short sessions with maggots, particles, pellets, groundbait and even floaters. If you have found the fish before you add any additional feed you should ask yourself what is the point of it? Will it make the carp more likely to sample your hookbait? Maybe make them more confident in your hookbait? Drop down in the water to find your hookbait? Maybe even stop them moving from your swim to someone else's? Get that carp brain into gear! And what if there is no visual sign of the carp and you are making an educated guess, or, even worse, an uneducated guess as to swim choice? Do you think that the carp will magically come to you because you are firing bait out? Probably more likely that you don't really know why you are doing it but that's what you do? Yes... me too and that's when it costs me fish... and no doubt you too. As I said at the start of the chapter ideas on bait application will be covered in some following chapters but do me a favour and stop and think logically about why you do what you do.... Of all the advice I am giving you in this book on short session success if you pick up on that and think 'why am I doing this?' you will soon become a much better carp angler.

Bait delivery for the purposes of this book falls into two specific areas firstly, bait to the hook and secondly, bait in the swim.

Bait to the Hook

This is where the additional feed you are applying is cast with your hookbait and to all extent and purposes your hookbait is sitting in a pile of that feed. You are casting out the feed with the hook which means you could not have it more accurately and compactly applied. This tends to be what I usually do when I am short session fishing, and the shorter the session the more likely I am to do this, and this alone. The less confident I am about my swim choice or the less I know about the water the more likely I am to keep it to hookbait feed only. These are the main items I use in bait delivery of this type.

Paste

The use of paste is a brilliant way to amplify the attraction of the hookbait you are casting out. Because the paste is not boiled there is no skin to seal in the attractors so the level of attraction around the hookbait is much more effective. Many bait companies make paste to match their readymade boilies, but if you are making your own baits simply save some of the paste you make your baits from. I tend to make a full mix up of the base mix that I would have rolled and simply make a couple of dozen tangerine-size balls of it. These are placed on a tray in the freezer and frozen solid. The night before your session take a ball out of the freezer and by the time you arrive at the lake the paste will be ready for use.

PVA Tape

The PVA stringer is an ideal way to get items of feed close to your hook bait. You can use both string or tape and the manufacturers now make it in winter and summer versions, thin and thick in diameter. Not only do stringers put that extra feed next to your hook bait but they are also ideal to stop tangles as the stringer will bounce the hook bait away from the mainline on the cast. You can use as few or as many items as you want and providing the item is dry it can be anything of your choosing. Whatever PVA tape or string you decide to use tank test it at home to check it works as it is supposed to do.

Below The PVA box is always with me in case I need string, tape, foam, mesh or solid bags for the swim I am in.

Bait Delivery: Tools and Approach

Mesh PVA bags

Popularised by Korda most of us have caught carp using the mesh bags. Again these are great in that once you fill them with whatever product you want you just nick your hook into them and cast it to the required spot. You can use them from thumbnail-size to as big as you can cast. Like the stringer they eradicate tangles too. Check how the PVA behaves when you fill and tie it, and as with PVA tape, all types, designs, sizes and meltdown rates are available for you to experiment with. You can also use mesh to fish a PVA stick – this is where you draw your hooklink through your filled mesh, a tactic known as the Dynamite Stick developed by the talented Nick Helleur. PVA mesh can be used with liquids that are not water-based so soaking them or dipping them in liquid foods can boost the attraction around the hookbait.

When using boilie crumb, solid bags are my first choice.

Solid PVA Bags

These too are an excellent way to have your hookbait sitting in the feed. Generally the lead and hookbait are placed in the bag to be cast out. The advantage of a solid bag which has your rig in it is that it can 'bomb' through the weed and as it breaks down your end tackle will be presented in a pile of feed and not snarled up in weed. You can add anything you want to it providing it's not water-based, which means you can pour in certain PVA-friendly liquids to attract the carp. Like the mesh bags you can use them any size you want. They are available in numerous designs but tank test them at home to see how yours behave.

I can't emphasise enough that the whole purpose of the paste, stringer or bag is to amplify the attraction of the hookbait, with the added benefit of the anti-tangle properties too. Providing you are on the fish and want to get that first one under your belt these methods are vital to practise and get right on short session fishing. The time to do it is not at the lake but at home, now. One afternoon with your favoured rigs and baits and the PVA being used as you'd cast them out will really open your eyes. Remember the percentage game? A tweak or two will improve your setup and results considerably.

Top Pellets are great but not so easy to deliver unless you master spodding, bagging... or buy a boat!!

Have spod will travel. Go and watch the BYCAC anglers at Linear and see how they do it. I did and I had to rethink and improve my efforts...

Bait in the Swim

In addition to the attraction of the hookbait and the paste/stringer/bag, you can also apply extra bait to the swim – with thought! Remember what I said at the start of the chapter? Why am I adding any additional feed other than the hookbait, and what will its effect be both positively and potentially negatively? You can always add more feed but you can never take it out. Bearing that in mind these are the tools of the trade:

By hand Up to a couple of yards you can apply bait by hand very accurately and very quickly. For marginal work it is brilliant but be very careful how much you put in; it is very easy to get carried away when not much effort is required.

Baiting spoon Firms like Nash and Gardner make excellent baiting spoons which you can either use to spoon bait in by hand, or attach to an extending landing net pole and tip the bait in. The Gardner model is perfect as it extends to almost ten feet and you can tip your free items and/or hookbait into position under bushes and suchlike where you would never be able to cast to, providing it is safe to do so.

Spods These really came to prominence in the 90s and most anglers use them to some degree. On some waters carp are drawn to the sound of the spod like a dinner gong sounding but on other waters, especially on short sessions, they can be the kiss of death, potentially moving carp out of an area. I tend to use them very infrequently on short sessions unless I want to short-cast a limited number of times with a small spod to get tiny feed items like maggots or particles in as soon as possible. You can, of course, use them for floaters too, but before you spod be aware of how much feed each spod-load is putting in and the effect it

will have on the fish you have in front
of you. If they are not in front of you
are you in the right swim, and are you
sure that the spodding will draw in fish
in the time you have? Similar to spods
are the Free Spirit Bait Droppers which
can deposit up to half a pint of bait at a
time but have the same disadvantages
that spods have on short sessions – the
disturbance factor.

Catapult The humble catapult is
something every carp angler should
possess but unfortunately many are
poor and many carp anglers use
poor techniques. The new ESP model
performs well but the catapults I use
I have made from separate products.
The frame is a bog-standard Drennan
Boily Pult, the elastic is pink Drennan
Groundbait Elastic and the pouch is

the famous Scruffy Bob version from the Tackle Box in
Kent. The pouch size depends on the type of feed and
amount of feed I put out. On short sessions I tend to use a
medium pouch and keep feed as minimal and as accurate
as possible. Like I said, with the hand delivery be careful
how much you put in. Practice makes perfect and to
be consistently accurate you must change your elastics
regularly. Something as simple as being accurate with
your catapult when you need to can, at times, be the line
between success and failure.

Top Catapults
incorporating Scruffy
Bob pouches from the
Tackle Box in Kent.
These are over five
years old and still
going strong. Need I
say more...

For putting boilies or
ball pellets out
at range the Fox
Carbon Stick has
done me proud.

Throwing stick Although many will claim
that they are accurate with a stick I see very few who are.
I tend not to use a throwing stick very often for short session
sessions other than to get small boilies out at range when
I am fishing my end tackle in a scattering of bait. At short
to medium range you will be far more accurate with a
catapult but if you need to apply bait further than 80 yards
and don't want to spod a throwing stick is a good choice.
You really need to practise, and having something like
an ESP Stalker Bait Pouch round your waist with the bait in
means you have the bait to hand and don't need to keep
bending down and losing your rhythm. My choice is a

I was tempted to pile in the bait, but as I had prebaited with Big Fish Mix, a single bait was all I needed to catch this mirror at dusk.

Bait Delivery: Tools and Approach

straight carbon throwing stick from Fox but you need to find one you are comfortable with and practise until it becomes second nature.

Bait Boats Personally I choose not to use them in my fishing but where they are allowed and you are comfortable using them, and can afford one, they are excellent for delivering as little or as much feed as you want together with your end tackle. Providing you know exactly what you are dropping your bait onto they are unrivalled when it comes to bait delivery, and for those of you with limited time, strong finances and the desire to use one they can be a very big advantage over those of us who choose not to.

Bait delivery is just one aspect of carp fishing but it is important to know what is available and how to use it properly. But most importantly, before you deliver bait you need to understand why you are doing it!

Chapter Ten
Boilies for Success

T hroughout this book aimed at the short session angler you will no doubt see that there is more to carp baits than boilies, with everything from the maggot to the wide array of imitation baits having their place in the tactics I describe. However, it would be daft to turn a blind eye to just how good boilies are, and despite all the alternatives they will probably form the main line of attack for much of your fishing – and why not ? You are not there to prove that you can catch on something other than a boilie, you are there to make the most of your time as quickly as possible.

With the increase in popularity of carp fishing the number of manufacturers making and selling boilies has gone through the roof and in all honesty it is hard to find a bad boilie if you stick to the proven firms. Firms cannot afford to make bad, or even average baits with all the competition there is around. I have been using boilies since Richworth Baits first brought out their neutral boilies in the mid 80's which you had to flavour yourself. Since then I have used boilies from most manufacturers and can honestly say that the ones I am about to detail I have caught hundreds, if not thousands of carp on, and hopefully will continue to do so. Rather than being a book about 'this product' and 'that product' I have tried to persuade the reader to use what you are confident in; only if it is not working for you should you consider changing in. Be it baits, rigs, tackle or tactics – if it ain't bust don't fix it.

Confidence is all-important in carp fishing so if you are happy with what you are doing then don't mess with that part of the equation and see if there are other areas you can boost your short session catch rate by. However, I know that some of you won't have the confidence that I have so hopefully the following boilies I recommend and use in spring, summer and winter will give you a good

Boilies for Success

starting point to work from. No heavy bait science, just details of the baits I use, and continue to use, and I can't be more honest than that. Virtually all of them you can buy off the shelf or, if in difficulty contact the firm as detailed via the reference chapter in this book. Some of the baits involve rolling them as detailed which you can do yourself, or you can get a reputable bait rolling service like Rollin' Baits to do it for you. As a short session carper you will not need a lot of bait and time is precious so if you have freezer space get it made for you. Time rolling baits is time you could have spent on the bank isn't it?

Nutrabaits Biollix. A totally underrated spring bait that will outfish many others!

Top **The wonderful Pineapple and Banana readymade. In spring it's my starting point.**

Spring

If you want to get bait that is already made then:

Nutrabaits Pineapple and Banana Classic Combination Shelf Life in 15mm

Richworth Shelf Life Tutti-Frutti ready-mades in 14mm

Richworth Midi Shelf Life White Chocolate ready-mades in 10mm

Heathrow Bait Services Pukka Pineapple Pop-ups in 12mm and 16mm

If you are prepared to roll your own then try:

Spring Mix One	Spring Mix Two
16 ounces of Nutrabaits Enervite Gold Base Mix	18 ounces Nutrabaits Biollix Base Mix
5 x Size 2 Eggs	5 x Size 2 eggs
7ml Nashbait Chocolate Malt Liquid Flavour	7ml Nutrabaits Liquid Kelp Extract
Heaped Teaspoon Nutrabaits Chocolate Super Sweet Powder	5ml Nutrabaits Caviar Flavour
1ml Nutrabaits Sweet Cajouser	12 drops Nutrabaits Black Pepper Essential Oil
Colour as required	25ml Nutrabaits CSL
	15ml Nutrabaits Hemp Oil
Roll 12-16mm and boil for 45-60 seconds	1ml Nutrabaits Sweet Cajouser
	No colour needed
	Roll 16mm and boil for 75 seconds

Summer

I tend not to use shelf-life baits but instead have them made as follows:

Summer Mix One

18 ounces Nutrabaits Big Fish Mix Base Mix

5 x Size 2 Eggs

5ml Nutrabaits Cranberry Flavour

30ml Nutrabaits Salmon Oil

1ml Nutrabaits Sweet Cajouser

No colour needed

Roll 16-18mm and boil for 75 seconds

Summer Mix Two

18 ounces Nutrabaits Big Fish Mix Base Mix

5 x Size 2 Eggs

25ml Nutrabaits G-Force Liquid

No colour needed

Roll 16-18mm and boil for 75 seconds

Summer Mix Three

18 ounces Nutrabaits Enervite Base Mix

5 x Size 2 Eggs

30ml Nutrabaits Nutramino

8 drops Nutrabaits Bergamot Essential Oil

1ml Nutrabaits Sweet Cajouser

No colour needed

Roll 16-18mm and boil 75-90 seconds

For single hookbait fishing the following are ideal:

Richworth Pineapple Hawaiian Airo Dumbell Pop-ups soaked in HBS Pukka Pineapple Reactor Dip

Richworth White Chocolate Airo Pops soaked in Richworth White Chocolate Impact Boilie Dip

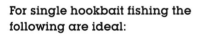

For single hookbait fishing, I will use glugs, bait soaks and dips like these.

Winter

When using shelf-life baits I'd choose:

Nutrabaits Strawberry Cream and Bergamot Classic Combination Shelf Life in 10mm and 15mm. Glug hookbaits alone in Nutrabaits Multimino

Nutrabaits Tecni-Spice Classic Combination Shelf Life in 15mm. To be used only as a hookbait and soaked for up to 18 months in Tecni-Spice Hi-Attract Bait Soak

Nutrabaits Pineapple and Banana Classic Combination Shelf Life in 10mm and 15mm. Hookbaits to be soaked in HBS Pukka Pineapple Reactor Dip for up to 18 months

Richworth Tutti-Frutti Shelf Life in 14mm. Hookbaits to be soaked in HBS Tutti-Frutti Reactor Dip for up to 18 months

Nutrabaits Trigga Ice ATS freezer baits in 16-18mm

Boilies for Success

So there you have the baits I consistently use all year round on a variety of waters. All of those will catch anywhere and, for me, bait is simply one part of the short session carping equation I do not have to worry about. I may consider how to apply, deliver and boost it but I never worry about the bait I am using. I know they eat it, and I urge you to build up confidence in your bait so that you too have that self belief. You do that by fishing a bait regularly, not by flitting about with bait, and using knowledge not hype to find and stick with a good bait.

The proof of the pudding is in the... Well I think you can see what I mean.

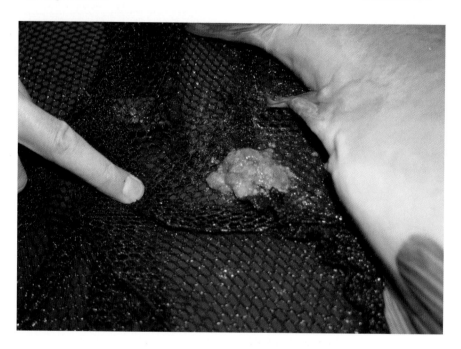

Chapter Eleven
Eyeball to Eyeball

f all the tactics within this book the art of stalking, once mastered, can catch you more than any other – once you put your mind to it. Throughout the book I describe the short sessions I normally fish as being anywhere from, say, 6 hours to under 24 hours, but when it comes to merely having a few hours at your disposal there is no better tactic to adopt than stalking. Not that it will work all the time, and not that it is effective on all waters, but if you are truly restricted for time, are prepared to be mobile and not follow conventional carping tactics this one is for you. It is you against the fish, and without reminding you of the obvious it involves walking round the water, looking for fish at close range and if, or when, you find them putting a bait to them so that you get a take within minutes rather than hours. It is frustrating at times when you can't find them, but when you do and get your approach right the rewards are there to be reaped.

Tackle

The best advice I can give to any angler who is going to adopt the stalking tactic is to have one rod and reel exclusively for this purpose. Unlike conventional carp fishing where you may be launching a PVA bag one moment and a method feeder another, with stalking you are generally fishing close in, so big reels and powerful rods are not needed, in fact, they will hinder you. I have a bog-standard Daiwa 12' AKN 2½lb test curve rod which must be all of 10 years old or more. Years of fishing have softened it slightly so that although it has the backbone to hook and hold it is less likely to pull hooks out on a short line. There are specialist stalking rods available from companies like Daiwa, Nash and Fox which are purpose built but if you have a spare rod and it has a degree of softness to it that's ideal. Reel wise I have a Daiwa Emblem 4500 which again is all of 10 years old, but perfect. The clutch must be silky smooth as carp hooked at close range can go ballistic and a clutch that is anything other than perfect can pop hooks out. The more solid and dependable the reel the better. It will end up being dropped on the floor, coated in mud and taking all sorts of abuse so it needs to be sturdy rather than trendy. It will need at least one spare spool, preferably two, so you can have the right line for the stalking situation you find yourself in. Main line wise it depends on the swim. Generally I use 15lb monofilament but I will go to 18lb in some circumstances. Mono has that cushion of stretch which makes it ideal for hook and hold at short range. Occasionally in clear waters there will be nothing to hide the main line so I use the X-line Fluorocarbon in 20lb which literally disappears underwater. As you are only using one rod carrying three spools is not that hard and as your end tackle will be pretty basic you can soon change spools without wasting time.

My rod and reel are housed in a rod sleeve which has written on it in bold black letters STALKING so that when I do go for my quick sessions I don't end up with the wrong one... whoops! Additionally, I take two small Gardner Stalking Sticks to put the rod on if I am not holding it, and the front one has my Neville buzzer on it and the rear one a rear grip which not only supports the rod but clamps it tight. Sometimes I don't even have a visual indicator but attached to the buzzer is the smallest Nash Slaphead bobbin, if needed. On most stalking sessions I am holding the rod but there will be occasions when the bait is in position and I am waiting for the carp to come back to the spot again. With the rod on the rests it is far more relaxing to sit back, watch for bubbles and that rod tip hooping over. With your one rod and reel combination you need to take the following, too:

- Landing net
- Unhooking mat (makes a great seat, too)
- Carp care kit
- Photographic gear
- Small bucket with whatever baits you are going to use and bait delivery tools
- Small bag with terminal tackle and accessories in it
- Small flask or water bottle and a few items of food

All that can easily be carried, no need for a barrow. If you are struggling to carry it you are taking too much…

Bait Again simple is best. You are only fishing for one carp at a time and although there will be times that you do introduce additional feed items, many of the carp I have caught stalking have been on single baits with maybe a small handful of feed around it. Your first job is to find where the carp are and, hopefully, feeding. You are not trying to get them to feed but putting a bait where they are feeding. I have a stalking bucket and inside it I usually take a variety of Dynamite Baits pellets, a tin of their corn, hemp and chopped tigers just in case. There's a small bag of Chum Mixers, some ready-made boilies and pop-ups, both visual and dark. The imitation Enterprise Baits products are in the tackle box and when I know a water well enough I do occasionally take maggots and worms.

Top Although I use a bright bait for stalking, sometimes a cubed dark one is the only way to get them to take it in shallow clear water.

The excellent Dynamite range of pellets and particles means I can use a little and often approach, without needing to prepare them myself.

The Korda Krusha is a must, and a small catapult just in case. On a water I am baiting regularly I would also take some standard boilies from the freezer, but no more than two handfuls. If the worst comes to the worst I can put them in as I leave but having them with me means I can trim them for hookbaits, crush them for a freebie or two, or crumb them if I am lowering a bag in.

Location and approach This of course is the key to success. If you go back to the chapter on observation and location I stress the importance to the short session angler of trying to find the carp before you set up to fish for them. There will be occasions when you can't find them and it is educated guesswork that puts you in a swim. With proper stalking that really isn't possible and unless they're exceptional circumstances where I have that rare 'sixth sense' moment where I feel carp will drift in, if I can't find them I often don't fish for them. That's not much

A gap in the bar to my right produced this stunner when the usual hotspots just were not delivering.

Although the rods are out to recognised hotspots, I'd baited the margins in front of me as I felt the carp would come in close at night.

use if you've travelled a long way, I agree, but stalking is just another tactic at your disposal not your ONLY tactic. If it's a very short session on a local water then it's no great hardship to walk, look and not find. Spending a couple of hours and not finding the fish and then going home needs to be looked at realistically. If you'd just turned up and cast out at the first swim you fancied would that have been any better? Doubtful! At least by looking you know that it was not to be that day.

When you have more time at your disposal you have to balance out the time spent looking to the time with your rods wound in. Again, unless you know where the fish are and they are out of stalking range and probably would respond better to conventional tactics the stalking approach is the right way to go. Looking for carp is never wasted time but casting out and waiting without a logical reason why you are doing it in that swim is. On busy waters stalking is not always possible but where you have a number of areas free from anglers and you have picked your time wisely it is.

Probably one of the best approaches when you really get to know a water is the baiting of swims approach. Now this is a little hard to try when it's a new venue or it's some way from home and there are other anglers when you get there. However, especially midweek in the summer when the carp come close in it's a great tactic to employ once you are in tune with the water. There will be areas that the carp favour and hopefully you will have seen them in those spots. By walking round the water and putting bait in these spots it really can be possible to draw carp into them.

Obviously carp are not going to swim from one end of the lake to the other to get to the baited spots, but if you use your commonsense you should be in the right area anyway. Think "Where would I be if I was a carp today?" Use your basic skills of location. They might not be in the spot now but in the time you have left will they turn up? A handful of pellets? Some chopped or crushed boilies? A carefully lowered spod or two of hemp and crushed tiger nuts? Just enough to get the carp to dip down, have a feed and for you to get your chance. Sometimes I will bait half a dozen such spots if I am sure the carp will be in these areas and that I have the time to benefit on my short session. Sometimes I am right, they are there and I catch one before I leave, and sometimes I am wrong and I go home fishless. But I always say would any other approach have worked better on the short time I had available that day? Probably not!

Technique Aggressive patience is the way I describe it. I am aggressive in my drive to find the fish but patient when it comes to fishing for them. I don't turn up at the water thinking it's stalking or nothing but when time is limited, or I am in tune with a water and start to get into the rhythm of it, then it is an approach I will adopt. Looking for them is the big deal. Be quiet, stealthy and accept that no spot is ever too close. If you have been conditioned to the bivvy and boilie approach it can be a culture shock but honestly, carp, big carp, can be found and caught feet from the margin. But unless you get into the mindset of trying it and believing in it you will never succeed. You will end up not looking properly, skimming, not observing and probably wishing you were sitting behind rods rather than putting the footwork in. That's okay but it's going to cost you and on short sessions you can't afford to miss out on such opportunities.

Let's say you've found the fish, what next? Well unless you really are running out of time catch your breath

Look carefully and you can see me fishing eyeball to eyeball.

and think your way into it. Keep as far back from the front of the swim as possible and observe what the carp are doing. They will tell you what they want to do not you dictating to them what you'd **like** them to do. The best stalkers are patient, watch the fish and reap the rewards. My friend Simon Crow calls it 'Heron Stalking' which is a great description. Watch a heron at work. It stands and watches, sometimes for hours, and then pounces. That should be you, too. Looking, watching and then catching. Sometimes you can observe what the carp are doing and what will trip them up in a matter of minutes. Sometimes it will take a lot longer. How are they behaving? What are they doing in front of you? Are they entering and leaving the swim a certain way? Dipping down on a spot? And so on… If possible as the carp drift in and out I will introduce a small amount of pellet or chops and see how they behave. Does it scare them? Do they start feeding? Once you've got your game plan then all you need to do is execute it.

Action Standing well back assemble your rod and use the appropriate rig. Mine are usually very simple and if I am not using a floating bait on the surface it will be a light running lead of under two ounces and a short hooklength to a bait of my choice. If the carp are still milling around don't drop the lead on top of them but wait till they drift to

one side to do that. A few grains of hemp carefully thrown into the area will sometimes get them to drift off. Landing net set up? Right, lower the end tackle into position and unless you are watching the fish and holding the rod, place it on the bank sticks and sit well back. Slack line, no need for a bobbin, and watch that line.

A scale-perfect common which came from under my feet when I couldn't get a take off the main bar which always produces... or so I thought!

When you hook the fish you must know what you are going to do, and do it. Are you going to hook, hold and bundle that carp in before it knows what it is happening, or can you let it run? You must think before you lower your end tackle or you may make a mess of your earlier hard work. Landing net in the right place? Now it's down to the carp and your patience. Don't be impatient and don't keep standing up and looking unless it is from a position you cannot be seen from. Keep quiet, bide your time and chill out. It may happen immediately, or it may take longer. However long it takes it will be worth it.

The stalking approach is ideally suited to readers of this book so go get that rod sleeve set up now and stop accepting the blank periods behind the rods. Ask yourself where those fish are, and how quickly can you get a bite from eyeball to eyeball fishing rather than watching a stationary bobbin.

Chapter Twelve
Spring: Now is the Time

lthough there is no specific definition of spring, for all intents and purposes when it comes to carp fishing I tend to view the period from March to May as spring. That to me is a time of year that the short session carp angler should try to take advantage of. In all likelihood you will have had to endure periods of inactivity in the winter and I guess some of you won't have wet a line for some time. Right, time to make a start and to make sure this year is one to remember with a successful spring. Although a carp fishing year is always twelve months long, from my own experience if I get it right in the spring months it bodes really well for the rest of the year. Carp under your belt will give you confidence, which tends to breed confidence. So even when it can sometimes be a struggle in the lethargic summer months you have your spring success to keep you motivated.

Venue
Although most venues can produce carp in the spring months I must admit that the best ones I have found for early action are shallow and weed free. Waters with depths in excess of ten feet can be notoriously slow to turn on and despite it feeling warm to us the deep waters just don't seem to switch on as soon as the shallow ones. I am not saying that temperature is the overriding factor – in fact, I think the hours of daylight are – but the shallower it is the sooner it warms up and the sooner the natural food will start to develop. Carp are creatures which thrive on opportunities and the more natural food the quicker they switch on to regular feeding. So if possible leave the deeper waters alone and look for a venue with a good percentage of the water being under 6 foot deep. Even if you have chosen a specific water for the year and it does

not satisfy this criterion, if you have not had any winter action to motivate you a trip to a smaller, shallower and more productive water can't do any harm. Getting back in the casting and accuracy routine, and practising your PVA bagging and self-take photography routine (more of which later) is a lot better if you are catching fish. Sitting at a 'big fish' water may well get you in tune with it but at what cost? Although I would always advocate trying to keep a consistent approach on one water some success in the spring should not be neglected. Waters that are weed free tend also to be more productive as the carp will have less opportunity to gorge on naturals over winter.

Planning

As always the more planning you put into the campaign the better. Unless I know a water really well I will visit it as often as possible in the winter months to get a feel for it even though I may not be wetting a line on it. My winter water will be satisfying my thirst for action but by visiting the spring water I can keep an eye on what is happening there. Are people already fishing it? Are fish getting caught at all? What about the presence of weed and the colour of the water? You don't have to wet a line to build up a mental picture of what is happening. Sometimes I even

take a rod with me so I can have a flick around with a lead to feel for weed, which can vary from year to year. Having a cold winter is not necessarily an indication that the weed will have been killed off for the spring and vice versa. Your eyes and a leading rod are better than guess work. Although there will be no magical 'turn on' date, as I said earlier I think it's more down to hours of light rather than temperature. At the end of February you start to approach the 12 hours of light/12 hours of darkness period which we call the Equinox. This is when I'd certainly want to start putting in as much time as possible. Occasionally odd fish will come out of the blue but if you start your main push when March appears on the calendar you won't go far wrong. Don't let me deter you from starting earlier as occasionally for some unfathomable reason an early February session will produce the goods. If you are a short session carper with some time on your hands give it a go.

Timing

Although carp will get caught in the hours of darkness in the spring virtually all my consistent action has come in the hours of light. Obviously if you have to travel to fish and can put in twenty four hours do so but try and get as much time during the daylight hours as you can. I am not

a great fan of weekend angling but in the spring I will fish
days at weekends if I can't secure a mid-week day off.
Putting overnighters in for overnighters sake can just drain
your confidence and no amount of hard work will persuade
them to feed in the dark if they are not ready to. Try to get
the daylight fishing in if you can. Again, although I do like
to fish for at least twelve hours, I have found that in the
spring, particularly early spring feeding spells, can be very
tight and if you can find the spot and the time you can
really do well. Sunday afternoons used to be great on a
number of my waters in the spring but as soon as the light
faded the carp would stop moving and feeding. Try to find
out when the carp are showing and feeding and even if it's
not you catching at first try to be there at those times.

Location

During the day I would start by looking in the shallows
especially if weed is present, be it old or new growth.
On some waters carp will lay up in the weed in winter and
a PVA bag in a dead weed bed or a Chod Rig feathered
down can produce the goods. Snags and reeds are my
next bet especially when the reeds are in water 2 feet deep
or more. I have seen carp laid up in the reeds in the spring

**Even with some ice
on the bank, once the
carp start to move and
feed in spring they are
more catchable.**

The Nash Diffusion leaders blend in on any lakebed.

in water which must have been cold but they seem to like the security of the reeds. If your water has islands in it, especially with overhanging trees and bushes, these two are right up there when it comes to getting bites. Most waters have areas that are sheltered from the cold northerly and easterly winds and when bushes overhang these protected spots you can often find numbers of carp laid up in the area literally for weeks on end. Any sun at all, especially in protected calm areas, is well worth investigating as carp do like the spring sun on their backs. The best location tip I can give you in spring which sounds too obvious to say but needs saying, is fish where they are. In the summer the carp will be on the move a lot more and even if you can't get on them there is probably a good chance that unless you really do get your location wrong fish will be in front of you at some time during the session. In the spring this is not the case and a miss is as good as a mile. Numerous waters will have swims which seem to produce the goods week after week and, unlike summer fishing, in spring I would say do whatever it takes to get in those swims. Weekends may well be a shut out but try to wangle a mid-week session if you can. It can take a lot of pressure to move these spring carp so if you can find them, get on them and milk it on your short sessions.

Tackle

If the weed has died off in the winter months fining down will get you more bites. Unless the water really is ultra-prolific with the fish colouring the water all year round, the water will probably be gin-clear a lot of the time so the more your end tackle blends in the better, so for me it's fluorocarbon main lines. I will try Diffusion leaders and anything I can find to blend in that end tackle. Even on day sessions I wouldn't dream of going without a brolly as conditions can change very quickly, even during the day. One moment bright sun and the next moment snow showers. If you've found the fish and are in the right swim set up the brolly anyway, but if you are on the move try to fish off the barrow. It will be cold so wrap up warm; take a flask and don't drain your energy and enthusiasm at this stage in the campaign.

Bait and Baiting

In the 'Boilies For Success' chapter I have detailed specific boilies that I have found to work well in the spring, but when it comes to bait I'd say use absolutely minimal amounts unless the water is very prolific and results have proved that more bait equals more fish. Even if that is said to be true I'd start very light and see how my results were in comparison to the anglers putting it in. My main aim in the spring, and especially on the short sessions I am putting in, is to get some carp under my belt not to necessarily to go for multiple catches. If you are on them single baits will do and extra bait will often not buy you more bites. If you are not on them a pile of feed is not going to get them over to your swim and get caught anyway. So single hookbaits with any extra feed being by way of PVA bags or PVA stringers is a good starting point.

Top When they start to move a good glugged bait can be a great starting point.

By using ball pellets I can put feed out at range without over feeding them.

The good old pineapple bait seems to work year in, year out, spring in, spring out, and most first bites of the year tend to come on such baits. However, if the water does get a lot of pressure sometimes using a pineapple bait in a colour other than yellow can be better. Most action will come in the day so the colour will stand out on shallow spots. I find home-made pineapple hookbaits in white or pink great alternatives when yellow has been done to death. Similarly, if most anglers are using pop-ups try a bottom bait in a bag of crumb. Trimming a pop-up till it just sinks or using a cubed bottom bait can be a winning method.

If I want to put some feed in I favour ball pellets as these break down very quickly, are easy to catapult accurately and can be glugged in an attractor of your choice. Remember you are not trying to get the carp feeding on your bait as such but to get them to make a mistake with the hookbait. Groundbait is another great method, and the sloppier the better. The attractors pouring out of it can stimulate the carp to feed and if the only solid item is attached to your hook it increases your chances of them picking up the hookbait. However, I would only put groundbait in where I thought carp were present as balls of groundbait on their own will not draw in fish. If you can find carp when stalking a bunch of maggots or a worm and boilie concoction make ideal hookbaits.

Although many anglers start their baiting campaigns in the spring unless I am the only one fishing the water I would not. Carp do not need educating to eat boilies and all sorts of bait will be thrown at them from now till spawning-time. Bide your time and save your bait. By all means trickle it in where you can see it being eaten to see how much they like it, but wait till they are spawning before you start to feed it in quantity.

Rigs

As with tackle the finer the better. Just because the carp may not have been active in the winter does not mean they will be stupid in the spring – far from it in fact. Clear shallow water makes crude or badly thought-out end tackles look very easy to avoid. I would fish as fine as possible and have the indicators as responsive as possible.

The infamous maggots or germs as some term them. I wouldn't be without them in March and April unless the nuisance fish were punishing me.

Spring carp do not always bolt off and I have had many just shake their heads as if they did not know what was happening or what to do. Spring is no time to experiment with rigs and just because you may have had a winter of reading and watching DVDs does not mean that the proven end tackles should be swapped for the latest wonder ones. Over light weed I'd fish a Chod and in heavier weed a solid PVA bag. On clear bottoms it would always be a fluorocarbon hooklength.

Spring: Now is the Time

Remember it will still be cold so do make sure your PVA does what it is supposed to. If the sun does come out carp may be susceptible to Zig Rigs so make sure you have the ability and items to fish that method. Carp may have spent a lot of time mid-water in the preceding months so don't miss out on that avenue, especially in periods of high pressure.

Tips and Tactics

Although you may be in a position to have a multiple catch on the right day in spring your approach should be geared to trying to get on the fish and winkle one out at a time. That means the minimum of bait and the greatest accuracy of delivery. If you do feel you are in the wrong swim and a carp shows elsewhere move to it. These spots where carp show can be very productive indeed. Spend as much time looking for fish as having a bait in front of them. You will find that if it is in the right spot at the right time action can come almost immediately. A sign of fish is most important so really spend time on your observation and location, not necessarily on bivvying up. Clear water should make them easier to see so if there are trees to aid observation use them to your advantage.

To me the spring is the gateway to my year but I have learnt not to push myself too hard. Many anglers will not have wet a line for months and from early March to early May the carp will be inundated with anglers, lines and bait. Don't kill yourself or your chances, don't use up all your holiday, and remember that the best time is still to come if you apply yourself properly.

Chapter Thirteen
Floaters: On Top Of Your Game

To be honest a lot of what I wrote about in relation to stalking applies to floater fishing too. The majority of carp anglers, me included, catch most of their fish on the bottom despite where the fish spend a lot of their time when we are pursuing them! Anglers who really work hard at their surface fishing do tend to catch more quickly than anglers simply fishing conventional methods based around fishing on the bottom. Having seen the likes of Chris Ball, Brian Skoyles and Jim Shelley in action I know that whether the carp are 14lb or 40lb they can, at times, be suckers for surface baits. The big problem with many anglers is that it requires you to step out of the box and work hard. No matter how much effort you put into bottom bait fishing generally when you have cast out much of the hard work is done and a lot depends on the carp. However, with floater fishing locating the fish is just the first stage; much of the hard work is still to come. Yes it does require effort but it can make carp fishing daft at times: it will catch you fish when nothing else seems to and, most important of all, it can allow you to be very selective as to the fish you want to take the hookbait. For those of us having to fish short sessions not only will it be, at times, the only way to get a fish but the way to get THE fish you want!

Venue

So you've chosen your venue anyway: what more is there to say? Well although some anglers will tell you that the water doesn't produce on floaters I have yet to find one that won't and, more importantly, my friends who fish countrywide say the same. If there are carp in the water be it Horton or Linear Fisheries you will be able to catch them on floaters. What is true to say is that some waters are more productive than others when it comes to floater fishing so

do bear that in mind. Because I am what I call an all-round angler I don't particularly choose a water because it's good for floaters, or stalking, but I'm always aware that these tactics are a string to my bow. Be they small or large I can almost guarantee that to you reading this your water will respond to surface baits.

I had carp taking Mixers like mad then these two had me pulling my hair out!

Mindset

As I have said in some of the earlier chapters self-belief inducing confidence can often be the difference between success and failure. If you turn up with the attitude that they won't take floaters – or, even worse, that you are not even going to try floaters – it can't work can it? It's not the method that's wrong it's your mindset my friend.

If your mindset is that they don't take floaters you won't try it. With the Gardner Rig Bins I literally just have to add a ready-tied floater rig on to prove they do.

I will admit from the start that I am not a great floater angler but because I have to try harder to make it work it can help me to point you in the right direction. Yes it is nice to sit back behind the rods relaxing but on short sessions is that the right attitude? Is that the most productive tactic? Come on, you know better than that! You have limited time so spend it to the best of your advantage and if it's floaters then get up and get motivated!

Time of year

It's easy to fall into the trap of believing that floater fishing is purely and simply a warm weather summer method. That's not so. Yes the carp do seem to spend more of their time on the surface in the warmer weather but I am sure that all year round they do spend a lot more time in the upper layers than the lower ones. If you can catch them on an anchored Zig Rig in mid December do you really think you can't catch them on surface baits in winter? So whether it's March, May or November when things are right and your approach is correct they may be catchable on the surface.

Tackle

Although you can catch them on any old rod and reel combination, unlike stalking floater fishing really does benefit from making a little more effort with your rod and reel. You may well be fishing at 10 feet or you may be fishing at 60 yards so it's important that you can cast that distance and strike into a carp that has not self-hooked itself. Some do but sometimes you are having to pick the line up off the surface and strike home the hook at ranges that are not all that easy to cope with. The rod needs to be light enough to hold for long periods of time, have a

Top By keeping the rod in a separate sleeve I am always prepared for opportunities.

The Daiwa Caldia X is perfect for surface fishing.

taper that picks up line quickly but is also able to subdue carp at close range. My choice is the Daiwa Infinity Barbel rod but I know that companies like Nash, Fox and others also make specialist rods for floater fishing.

As with the rod the better suited the reel the more effectively you will fish. Too big and the setup will be imbalanced but too small and you may not hit the distance. My choice is the Daiwa Caldia X which combines lightness and, most importantly, a beautifully smooth clutch. You may be using a main line as light as 6lb and a hook size 10 or 12 so it is important that the clutch is silky smooth as you lead rather than bully the carp in. Main line will depend on where I am fishing. Generally it's 10lb but I do have a spool in 12lb for weedy water work and a spool in 8lb for fishing at range.

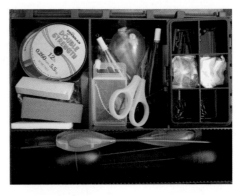

As with stalking the rod and reel combination goes in a separate rod sleeve marked FLOATER on it so I can't make any mistakes. Unlike stalking, which is something I tend to set out to do, floater fishing tends to be something I will do if I feel conditions are right. Yes, from time to time I will wander round a water with my floater gear, but usually my floater sleeve always goes with me summer and winter alike as part of the armoury of gear that sits on the barrow. What I do have is a small box of floater accessories that fits inside the rod sleeve so I am never without the exact items I need to surface fish. The box contains controllers, hooklengths, hooks, imitation baits and anything I need to catch them off the top. Not being prepared is inexcusable really!

Calm Water/Over Weed Controller Setup

Basically, the controller lays flat, which means you can move it about on the surface with minimal disturbance. Because of this setup's low profile, it is ideal to use over weed.

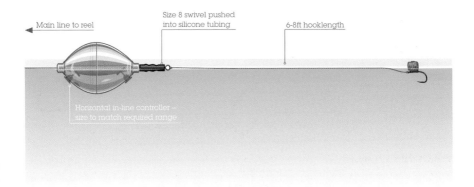

Main line to reel

Size 8 swivel pushed into silicone tubing

6-8ft hooklength

Horizontal in-line controller – size to match required range

Windy/Long-Range Controller Setup

This setup is ideal for conditions where you need to hold the bait in position. Having the bulk of the controller underwater allows you to control the position of the hookbait.

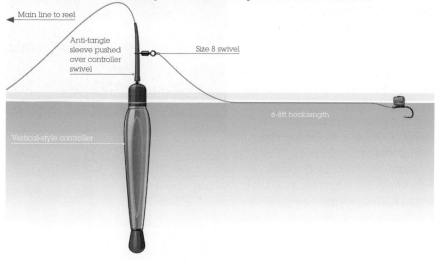

Main line to reel

Anti-tangle sleeve pushed over controller swivel

Size 8 swivel

6-8ft hooklength

Vertical-style controller

Surface Presentations

These are the three methods I use to attach a mixer-type bait to the hook. Generally I use a Drennan Double-Strength hooklength of 6-8ft, and a size 10 or 12 Korda Mixa hook.

Basic Knotless Knot presentation

Reverse Hair Presentation

Stretch Band Presentation

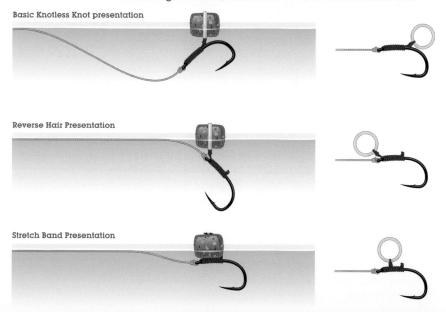

Bait

Well if it floats the carp will take it, I guess! However, if you never used a different bait again and stuck to the humble dog biscuit Chum Mixer you would catch a lot of carp, and I mean lot of carp. There are numerous baits that will work apart from Mixers and in my floater bag of baits I have floating boilies, some excellent Enterprise floating baits and a variety of specialist floating pellets. Occasionally I will add a soak to my mixers such as the Nash Crustacean soak or Nutrabaits Salmon Oil but my aim is to get the carp past the point of no return in a feeding frenzy so that a specific bait is not really the big issue.

Top Standard Mixers are fine for most waters.

Flavoured Chum Mixers will outfish standard one as Brian Skoyles proved to me. Hey I am a believer Bri...

Location

Unlike stalking where you really are looking for carp to just a few feet out, floater fishing can be done from the edge to as far out as you can cast and present a bait. I have caught carp at well over 60 yards with surface baits but the closer in the easier it is. If they self hook that's great but otherwise you are lifting the line to pull the hook home. Don't make it any harder than it needs to be but don't restrict your range either. If I can see or find carp on the surface then they are catchable is my motto. There is an area where stalking and floater fishing are one and if you look at what I wrote in the chapters on observation and location and the one on stalking you will see how they all interact. If you find carp at close range on the surface then make sure it's the surface bait you use. They will take it either lowered to them or by building up their confidence with a steady trickle of surface baits. Patience and application will get you results. One of the little tricks I have in locating carp on the surface is when I am static fishing behind my rods or wandering round baiting stalking spots I will trickle in floaters here and there. Sometimes you will see or hear a floater being taken when there really was no visual evidence to suggest the carp were in that area at all. Waterfowl can make this problematical – if not impossible – at times, but if they are not a problem then trickling in the Mixers, especially on short sessions, can reveal carp when your eyes couldn't locate them.

Tactics

Casting out my floater rig is always the last part of the game plan and if you have got it right you can get a take in seconds or minutes. Yes, that quickly. Let's say you have found fish and they are on the surface. What next? Well as I always say catch your breath, don't panic or rush things and you will be fine. If you have found them because they've found your trickle of Mixers that's great. If not you need to see how they feel about the floating baits on the day. Sometimes just one or two will spook them never to return yet on other days you can pepper them constantly and get them going crazy – that's carp on top! If they are simply there but not taking I will use my catapult and fire some beyond or to the side of them. Not too many, maybe just a pouch or two. Sit down on the unhooking mat and observe. Floater fishing is very much a waiting game but at least you've found them. The rod and reel are still in the sleeve and the net has yet to be unfolded. I am letting the carp tell me what they want to do and what they are prepared to put up with. It may only be a short session but I will know what time I have and applying logic will tell me whether this is good use of it.

If I have found carp on top and the odd Mixer is disappearing the omens are good. Sometimes it does not happen but let's presume it is happening. If the odd Mixer is going trickle a few more in and see what happens. Sometimes this can take minutes and sometimes it can take up the bulk of your short session: that's the unpredictability of carp fishing. Once they do start taking generally it's a sign that they are catchable – if I don't muck it up. I will continue to feed in Mixers until I am pretty sure I know how many carp are in front of me and that they are starting to compete for the Mixers. Then and only then will I set my rod up. By now I will know how far out I need to be and what tackle I need to land the fish. Line threaded, float added and correct presentation chosen. Landing net up and keep the Mixers going in. If you have got things right the carp will be really competing for the food on the surface with swirls everywhere. The trick is to build up this state of competition until the carp are literally past the point of no return. They are just concentrating on the food items and not the possibility of danger. This is the time you should add your hookbait to the party. If you cast before this point you may get a take but in all likelihood you will end up spooking the carp and chasing them out of the swim. Providing you have plenty of Mixers to keep adding it is literally impossible to be too late to the party! Over cast and draw the float and bait in, then let the carp do the rest. Wait till the hookbait is taken, the line tightens and you strike the hook home. Game on – or is that game over!

Floater fishing is an important tactic whether you fish short or long sessions. The great thing is that many anglers are too lazy and poorly equipped to do it properly. Providing you have the tackle and the mindset as I described you can build up the swim without wetting a line until the last possible moment, really putting the 'short' into short session success.

Surface fishing – don't miss out!

Chapter Fourteen
Night Time Is The Right Time

Some 20 years ago when I really got into my carp fishing I realised that to keep a balance in my life something was going to have to suffer. Much as I loved my carp fishing weekends were also for spending time with my girlfriend, friends and family and to chill out after a full week at work. Worse still, with carp fishing getting ever more popular every man and his dog seemed to want to turn up on Friday night and go home on Sunday. Not only was I not getting a good choice of swim but on some occasions I wasn't getting a swim at all. So what could I do? Well I could complain and whine about it not being fair or I could do something about it.

To start with I would go straight from work midweek, fish well into dark and then go home. That caught me quite a lot of bonus fish midweek but I also seemed to be spending a lot of time travelling, setting up and packing up compared to the hours I was actually fishing. So rather than do that I decided I'd see what it would be like to fish the night after work and then go to work the next day. I remember that first night was a bit of a shambles as I had not got anything to go on and although I caught a double, going straight to work after that was not going to make me popular with the office staff. I stepped back, thought about it and over the next few years began to fine-tune the tactic until I had got it to a level where I felt it was benefiting my carp fishing hugely without impacting too negatively on my day-to-day life. It wasn't easy for me then and it won't be easy for any of you reading this who are about to try it, but it will be a lot easier if you follow the advice I give. Everything I get right nowadays I got wrong previously so please don't think it falls into place just as I write it. You will make mistakes, you will feel tired, but if you put the effort in your catch rate will be so much better,

Night Time Is The Right Time

I promise. Fancy catching a lot more carp this season and beyond? Well read on…

The first point is that doing overnighters is not simply just doing nights as you would on a weekend or on a longer session. Overnighters for the short session angler require a great deal more planning and self discipline but at the end of the year you will have a lot more carp to your name. Providing you are not neglecting your family or work it's a heck of a way to 'create' fishing time when there appears to be none available. If you are going home and just watching the television, going to the pub or just chilling you can turn that time into opportunities in your carp fishing. Heck if you have a partner they may well prefer you to fish midweek so that come weekends you can become a normal human being again rather than the person who is never home at weekends. Overnight carp fishing may well save your marriage – but don't blame me if it does!

I'll emphasise that you really do need to pick the right water for the time you can realistically devote to your fishing, which in this case is an overnighter. Ideally it would be a water that you could go to directly from work, and when you pack up in the morning go straight to work from it. Now that's okay if it fits round your work schedule but for me it wouldn't. I have a job working in the court so I do need to be clean and tidy at work which inevitably means a bath, hair wash and so on. Yes I do lose around an hour each way but I can live with that because of the extra fishing I get in and keeping my job. In my case then I need a water no more than an hour from my base and work, preferably a bit closer. The closer it is the quicker you can be there and be home, but go back to the earlier chapters to remind yourselves of the points you must consider.

Once you have picked your water it is important to know the habits of the other anglers which again I covered in the Make the Most of It chapter. I know all waters are different but I'd hazard a guess that the best two nights for you to target are Sunday and Wednesday. Sunday nights are usually quiet on many venues and by Wednesday you may have caught up on your sleep! As you get into the flow you may decide to fish two nights in a row to maximise what you

The alarm clock was set for 4.30am. Could you do it week in, week out?

My living quarters for many nights from March through to November. It isn't flash but I am there to catch carp.

learnt on the first night but that will only come once you are used to the self-discipline of doing overnighters. I tend to be very fluid in my approach, using Sunday nights as a starting point and then playing it by ear as to which other night I do, if any. When I am in tune with the water I may do two midweek nights as well but if not I will only do one to not overstretch myself. Fishing is not compulsory and you should recognise the difference between pushing yourself and going for going's sake. That too will come in time but start on a Sunday night if possible and consider Wednesday's too if you are up to it.

Once you arrive at the water – and let's say it's late Sunday afternoon – as it's your first overnighter you need to consider where you should be. Unfortunately that's not as simple as saying fish where the fish are because you are spending the majority of your time fishing the hours of darkness. It's not just a case of where they are when you arrive but where they will be during the majority of your session. On a water where you'd be lucky to get a fish, if you find them and can avoid spooking them that's a great place to start. However, if it's not that difficult a venue you need to pick a swim the fish will be in during the hours of darkness and where you can realistically expect to land them and get a bait back out. Some swims you may be able to winkle one out in the day but in the dark it may be just plain dangerous to fish and will lead to untold frustrations for you.

If I see fish and I have time to go for them then I will. In the summer months I do have a floater rod set up in one of my rod sleeves and it really is just a case of using this off the barrow. You have to weigh up the time pursuing the fish in this swim compared to the time you are losing in perhaps a better overnight swim. There are areas of the lake carp will prefer in the day and areas they will prefer at night so you have to use your carp brain to consider where your time is best spent. An experienced angler may well be able to fish a swim or two before settling in for the night but a less experienced overnight carp angler would best be advised to set up where he thinks the carp will be that night.

So you've picked your swim, taking account of the advice I gave in my earlier chapters, now what? If carp are crashing out all over the place in front of you it may well be sound advice to get the rods out immediately and I for one would. As long as my landing nets are assembled and the unhooking mat is down then get a bait on them straightaway so you don't miss out. But what if that isn't happening, as is the case on many of the sessions I fish? Carp are present; I am sure this is the swim to fish the night in but do I need to get the rods out that minute? In a word... no! Take a minute or two to weigh up the situation. Is this swim suitable for the night? What is the weed like? How about snags? If you hook one can you land it? When you've landed it can you get the bait into position again? Those are musts in my book and the closer in I can fish the better! 10 yards is better than 30 yards and 30 yards is a lot better than 60 yards and so on. It can be hard enough to catch them at night without making it any harder with the wrong choice of swim.

If you are satisfied that it is the right swim then I'd urge you to get organised before you get the rods cast out. What I am about to detail may take a little time to describe but from arriving in a swim and catching my breath I can usually get my shelter up, stuff sorted and rods ready in well under 20 minutes. Personally I can live with that so I am organised and not all over the place but you need to decide how important it is for you to get the rods out immediately.

I couldn't get in my first choice of swim, so instead I fished all three rods to one spot in my second choice swim, to maximise my chances.

Firstly I get my shelter up which is usually an open-fronted umbrella system like the Nash Oval Plus or Daiwa Mission system. There is never a front attached as I want to be able to see the water from the shelter without having to look round a door. I tend to put the shelter to one side of the swim if possible so that I am not in obvious view of the fish and my casting and playing is not obstructed by the shelter. I peg it down with the T-pegs rock-solid and use a trimmed down groundsheet to keep everything dry. Rods are assembled and then placed to one side of the swim. Both nets are assembled and again placed to one side of the swim. As much of this work as possible is carried out well out of view of the swim by using the trees and bushes to disguise my movements. Bedchair out of the bag, sleeping bag on it and all the rig gear, including rig and PVA boxes, on top of it. The rest of the stuff is left in the barrow bags or inside the empty bedchair bag. That my friends has taken no more than five minutes!

Night Time Is The Right Time

I catch my breath again and decide where I want to place my end tackles. Walking round earlier and using my commonsense has probably already given me an idea so it's a case of pushing in the bank sticks and lining up the rods on each of the setups. Rod mats down to protect the reels and visual indicators if need be, I then start to think my way

into the session. Once I've decided where to cast and how much bait to use then out go the rods with the lines being marked and the sight lines and plan being drawn. I tend to use few, if any, free offerings unless of I am fishing a prolific water where a quantity of bait helps. I'll maybe introduce a scattering of free offerings or a spod or two of bait in the area but when in doubt, I keep it out. The more I get to know the water the more I will know when and when not to apply the bait. You will too! Go light to start with and experiment as I detail in the Multiple Hits chapter later in the book. On many waters I am trying to catch one as soon as possible and build it up from there.

Baits out, indicators and buzzers on, I sort out the rest of the gear. The cooking gear is minimal and I take just enough food to stop me feeling hungry and lethargic. Most of the gear fits in the two barrow bags so that the swim outside and inside the shelter is as organised as possible. The unhooking mat is set in position, the camera set up for self-takes and at last I can relax with my first hot drink and biscuit or two. Game on! Sounds a lot of messing about but honestly once you get into a routine it's a bit like driving. You get somewhere but you don't remember the journey! On overnighters I just click into that mode and before I know it I am sitting on the bucket cushion with the hot drink ready for that first take.

Before the light fades you must be prepared for the night ahead with organisation being your friend and carelessness your undoing. Landing net on either side of the swim and a torch in front of the rods if you need it. Are you sure you can hit the same spots in the dark if need be? Are the sight lines visible in the dark as well as in the light? Gear under cover in case it rains? Shelter rock-solid and all the essentials to hand? I have a little tub I keep my car keys, alarm clock, phone etc. in so I don't lose them. I also make sure my other essentials like rig boxes, Fox Box and PVA holder are on top of the barrow bag for use when I need to rebait after a fish. I also have a gas lamp to use when necessary. Providing you are not shining the light into the water and you are not disturbing other anglers I see nothing wrong with that additional light source to help when rebaiting, photographing fish and so on.

I tend to stay up as late as I can and if you refer back to the observation and location chapters you will see why – the hours from dusk to dawn are the best time to see the carp. If I see fish showing consistently in a spot that I feel is better than where my rods are currently positioned I will redo at least one rod to that spot. Obviously it is a balance. How comfortable are you with what you are casting at? What was wrong with your original positioning? Will it scare the carp in the swim, and so on? Don't chase carp round unless you do it logically and it's better than doing nothing.

Occasionally I will move in the hours of darkness if I really feel I need to but again, this is a balancing act. Is the move really worth it? Can I do it without making a real mess of things? Will I be able to set up in the dark? How will it affect me when I have to pack away and so on? It's very easy to trot out about moving swims at night but for the purely overnight session angler it is not always the best thing to do. Once I am happy I can do no more and need to sleep then I will do so. Unless I am wearing contact lenses my glasses are clipped on the chain round my neck so that I don't forget them when I run out to strike a fish and that way they don't steam up. There will be nothing between me and the rods so sleep calls…

Whether you catch or not, at some point the next morning you will have to leave for home or work. As I start work at 9.00 a.m. I tend to be off the water no later than 7.00 a.m. so I can get home, wash and get to work without being daft on the roads. It takes me no more than 30 minutes to pack down so I really need to start packing down 6.00 to 6.30 a.m. Of course you need to work out your own time scale. What I tend to do is always get up a least one hour before I have to pack up, sometimes a lot earlier, to look for fish. There is nothing worse than simply waking

up and packing up. Normally the alarm clock goes off around 4.45 a.m. and I start my day again. Sometimes I will rebait with an alternative hookbait to try for a bite but usually I just try to gather my thoughts. Plenty of coffee helps. I will not recast unless I have to but bit by bit, as silently as possible, the gear is packed down. If it's a water I am fishing and baiting regularly out will go my freebies so that next time the fish will hopefully be even more confident. The rods come in second to last with the landing nets in last. Check nothing has been left and back to the car with that loaded barrow.

Overnighters are not easy and they do take some getting used to. Most of my overnight angling is from early April to late October so that I can arrive during daylight which does make it a lot easier. Even after 20 years of doing overnighters the first couple each year are hard work and tiring, but once I get my body in tune to that style of angling it can be done. If I can do it you can too. Make it happen because it certainly won't if you just sit at home bemoaning your lack of time to go carp fishing.

Hangin' on, hangin' on, just in case! On short sessions, every minute counts.

Chapter Fifteen
Summary: You Only Need A Few Hours

f all the seasons for the short session angler the period from early May to late September is a time when the length of session can be unimportant but application of effort most important. Many of the anglers who fish longer sessions will probably have been at it since March, and although they may well have had some good catches on more pressured waters, the carp soon learn to avoid the 'same old, same old' approach that longer sessions inevitably breed. It's something that you can slip into when you are fishing longer sessions I'm afraid. It worked before so I will just set up, cast out and my chance will come. Well often in time it does, but as a short session angler you really can reap the rewards – even on the briefest of sessions – by doing something different. All it takes is a little self belief that you are not hampering yourself by the shorter sessions and the drive to keep mobile and free thinking. Summer is your time so make it happen.

Venue

As your plan should be to fish as many sessions as possible rather than longer ones, a venue close to home is probably still your best bet. The summer months will have periods where waters seem to turn off to 'conventional approaches'. Although I would normally advise to you stick to one water, if you have a number of local ones this is even better. Being able to pick the right venue at the right time is an attribute you will develop if your time is to be put to best effect. Conditions really can make a difference, and so can angler pressure. For instance, one of my waters always fishes well on red-hot calm days, but only in one area. If I can't get in that area I tend to visit another water. Once you get to know your venues you will develop a rhythm and be able to predict which water

Rods out and kettle
on. This night most
anglers were away on
holiday and I had the
lake to myself.

you are best targeting for the time you have available. Flogging yourself to death, even on short sessions, on one water alone is not good angling I assure you. You must consider what your targets are, too. If it's regular captures before winter then pick a prolific water. If it's one particular fish then do your research as to when it usually gets caught. If you know what you want you can pick the right venue for yourself. If you don't how can you?

Planning

As I said earlier many of the longer session anglers will have been hard at it since March and you can make this work to your advantage. Look at the swims. Which ones have seen constant angler pressure and which ones are less popular? What is the angler pressure like? Anglers will start to find their own patterns and tend to fish certain days, certain times and sometimes certain swims. Once you know your fellow anglers' plans you can fit yours round them. Some waters may be packed on Fridays and Saturdays but empty on Sundays. Some are busy towards the end of the week and quiet midweek. Think about holiday periods and when other anglers usually take theirs. There is no point arranging your fishing when your swim choice is going to be dictated by other anglers, is there? Plan your time wisely but only when you know what you have to contend with. I tend to save my holiday time for later in the year as there are plenty of daylight hours to fish in during the summer anyway. Holiday time is saved until when the clocks change and it's dark late afternoon. Planning is more than just what you are doing there and then.

Timing

Even in this country there are often periods of settled warm weather and although waters may well fish in the day the dawn and dusk periods seem to rule the roost for many anglers. The period from dusk to dawn will see a cooling of the water and generally that is when the carp will feed strongest. If you can't do overnighters then don't panic because carp can be caught during the day providing you time your approach sensibly. Unlike spring and winter when the carp tend to feed in very defined feeding spells, in summer I would be confident that somewhere on the water a carp will be catchable providing I get my approach right. Sitting behind rods won't necessarily be the right approach and that's why your short session tactics will prove beneficial. What time have you got? Where would you expect the carp to be during that time? Where are they? Not as hard as some make it out to be. The only time I really do take time off work for fishing, if possible, is after spawning. Once carp have spawned they will feed strongly to repair themselves and build up energy. If I see carp spawning it does not deter me like it deters some. I know that if I get my timing right multiple catches are possible.

Location

Where are they? In a word anywhere... and I mean anywhere! If a water has weed then you can bet it will be at its thickest in the summer. Carp tend to shoal up a lot less and although there may well be prime swims, the carp will probably be well distributed around the lake. A lot of anglers like to fish nights and tend to select swims where they can comfortably fish during darkness, although that's not always where the fish are, of course. They are where they are and you need to find them and decide whether you can safely land them. The more weed there is, the closer in they will come. Remember what I said in the Observation and Location chapter? It's important to find them rather than decide in advance where you'd like them to be. Carp love the shallow water in the summer and although the longer session anglers will leave it alone ('I wouldn't do a night in there mate') you only need a few minutes to make it happen. The more pressured a water is the less likely they are to follow a wind, but if you have the time always check the area a new wind is blowing into just in case. Summer is about looking in all the nooks and crannies that others miss out on and pinching a fish here, there and everywhere rather than banging away in the same old way.

When the weed thickens up I tend to up my line strength.

Tackle

If the weed is up you simply have to upgrade your tackle to cope with it. In the summer I will think nothing of using 18lb main line and size 4 or 6 hooks if the situation demands it. You think the hook looks crude and big in your hand? Well that's not where you are casting it is it? Think about it presented in the weed...

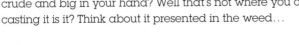

size **4**
barbless

not so obvious then is it? Most of my summer fishing is on a mobile basis so I tend to take the minimum of gear and move if I have to. Don't compromise yourself by not taking your floater and stalking gear. Much of the time I will fish off a barrow and if I am doing an overnighter I will not set up the shelter until I am sure that I am in the right swim. On some nights I will not even set up a shelter so that I can spend more time fishing and less time setting up and packing up. You are not boring them out but finding them, fishing for them and moving on.

Bait and Baiting

I am not afraid to use bigger hooks in heavy weed.

The carp were gorging themselves on natural food so I had to find a way to get them on my feed.

Although I do tend to use the baits I have detailed in the 'Boilies for Success' chapter at times in summer the carp can show less inclination to make a mistake with the hook bait. It's not that they are not eating the boilies but not feeding strongly enough to make a mistake with the hookbait. Alternative hookbaits really are worth a go and from maggots to tiger nuts, bread flake to the pop-up and worm combination you should not rule out anything. The carp will have had months of constant pressure and with safe natural food to gorge themselves on the boiled bait approach is not always the best approach for the short session angler. If I was fishing a water regularly I would

still put the bait in as I left but not cut down my chances by overfeeding them when I'm fishing. The 'baiting as you leave' approach is hopefully making your future fishing easier. If I am using boilies then small bags of crumb with the boilie and tiger hookbait approach can be a winner. Floaters should never be neglected so brush up on that tactic. Anglers fishing longer sessions, especially on weedy waters, seem loath to wind in rods which have taken time to position so make that pay for you. Floaters can be fired all over the place to make location even simpler. You may not find them but they will find the floaters and then you have your clue as to where to fish. If fish are up in the water any 'oily' approach will work well. Groundbait with plenty of liquid is great for putting in holes in the weed to get the carp to drop down to feed. Forget the beds of boilies and use bait sensibly, not just in piles.

When I fish a single bait in summer, I often glug it for maximum 'find me and eat me' signals.

Rigs
This can be a little more problematic as you have to balance subtlety with strength. You have to use rigs that allow you to land the fish but aren't crude, this will prevent the carp which have been hammered on them for months becoming intolerable of them. One tip is to watch what others are doing and see how you can improve on that.

I sometimes just carefully lower a few spods of hemp in and fish a single tiger nut over it when the water temperatures are high.

Many anglers will be flogging the same tactics to death so use some fine-tuning to improve your chances. That could be going very short or very long with your hooklength. If it's weedy the leads must discharge on the take and if in doubt about any item of tackle, change it. Weed and sunlight plays havoc with line so keep checking it. When you wind in let the line pass through a cloth in your fingers so excess silt and weed do not thicken up your line unnecessarily. Whether you are stalking or floater fishing, bottom baits or Zig Rigs when the fish takes the rig needs to be 100% efficient. If not it will cost you.

Tips and Tactics

Although the more time you have the better, any time can be productive during the summer. For many anglers the summer period is when they too have to fit in family activities. Add to that spawning, lethargic carp, bog-standard tactics not working and it's not surprising that on some waters the pressure decreases not increases. Anglers who can keep it together will benefit providing they use commonsense. The bivvy and boilie approach may well work at other times of year but if it's not the one in the summer don't do it. You need to tailor your approach to the situation you have, not to what you'd like it to be.

Summer: You Only Need A Few Hours

The carp are likely to be mobile and so should you. Heat, mosquitoes, carp not playing by the rules… Not as easy as the books make it out to be, eh? But that's wonderful news for the short session carper who adapts each and every time. It is a lot easier to change your approach on shorter sessions than it is during longer ones… because you have to. To me each short session is a new start and no amount of work is too much. It can be hard work and sometimes you will have to push yourself but the rewards will come.

Dynamite Hemp. It's not called Dynamite for nothing!

Summer is often written about as the 'best' time to catch carp, but it can also be the most difficult of times to catch them. Make the limited time you have pay and hopefully you will find that as winter approaches you've just had your best season ever.

Chapter Sixteen
Under Pressure:
The Weekender's Lament

I n an ideal world as a short session angler looking to catch consistently you'd try to select the best possible times for your fishing and, without doubt, weekends don't usually fall into that category! From the very start of the rise in popularity of carp fishing weekends have been pressure time: many anglers work during the week with weekends being the only chance to get out and fish for carp. From the very start of my carp fishing this is what I had to contend with, too, but in later years I found that overnighters were probably more productive with the time I had free to me. However, I still regularly fish short sessions at weekends as many of the waters I target simply don't produce at night. So if I want to catch one then weekends it has to be. No doubt many of you fall into this category too? You'd prefer to fish when it was quieter but if the weekends are all you've got it's then or nothing! With that in mind this chapter will hopefully help you to get the best from weekends, providing you believe in yourself.

Weekend angling for the short session angler tends to fall into two distinct areas. There is either the 24-hour session angler, or the 'Let's fit 12 hours or so in when I can' carper. Of course there are those who can fish from Friday through to Sunday, but although there will be tips they too can learn from this, but if your fishing is based on 24 hours or less then start reading and putting what follows into practice. If you are at the mercy of being dropped off and picked up at a certain time it becomes even harder still, but don't worry, you can still do it. You will just have to work harder to keep on top of your game

Ignore Fridays

Most anglers who fish the weekends, or one weekend night, tend to start on a Friday night, especially in the summer months when it is possible to travel to a water, set up and cast out in the light. Unless I had to I really would give Friday nights a miss as pressure will be at its highest. Although you may find a swim free it is very likely to be nowhere near the ideal area. However, if you have to arrive on a Friday and are facing this choice, and want to have the luxury of a full weekend at it no matter where you fish, I would take the minimum amount of kit so that if anglers leave on Saturday, or the carp are moved to quieter areas because of the pressure, you can move very quickly. Literally you will be using that Friday night to fish single baits and hoping that your observation and location skills help you move onto the carp whilst the other anglers are still asleep, or on their way home.

A popular water in winter, so I had to up my game.

Friday Night/Saturday Morning

If you have the luxury of 24 hours to play with then – if the water allows it – I would recommend not racing down on Friday night but instead turning up between midnight and 2.00 a.m. and then making your decision as to where to fish. Those who are going to fish will already be set up and the carp will have already been subjected to the repeated

Not a favoured corner swim but I felt that the weekend pressure would have pushed the carp into it.

casting of marker floats, leads and spods and a mountain
of bait being fired in, usually for no logical reason. I often
find that this onslaught completely kills Friday nights stone
dead and any carp that are going to show will do it well
after midnight and into the dawn period. Load your gear
onto the barrow and make your way to the best place to
watch the water for fish. Go back to the chapter I wrote on
observation and use that period from midnight to 6.00 a.m.
to give you all the clues you need. If it were me, once I'd
seen signs of movement I would move into the appropriate
swim, fish single baits only and literally fish off my barrow
in case I had to move again if a better swim came free.

Saturday

If you can't get to the venue until Saturday morning then
it is vitally important that your swim choice is not rushed: a
mistake at this stage really can ruin the whole session. The
swims that will be left will obviously not be first choice swims
– unless your fellow anglers are really slow on the uptake
– but remember, that after the Friday night barrage what
may have been a great swim on Friday afternoon could
well be a poor swim now. And what may not have been a
good swim at that time may well be worth a look if the carp
have moved away from the angler pressure.

   Although I usually try to avoid filling my head with
opinions as to what the anglers present think at a time like
this, I really want to know as much as possible as to what
the situation is. Has anything been caught last night? You
often don't even need to ask as wet nets and mats will tell
you that, and thankfully most anglers will be only too proud
to tell you. You can look at where the other anglers are
fishing and, most importantly, what their tactics are. Again,
you don't need to blatantly ask, just use your eyes. The
important thing is if very little has been caught, why? Is it
because the water is 'off', or is it that the angler pressure has
pushed the fish into other areas? Think like a carp and you
will succeed. If you were a carp today where would you be?
I wouldn't be in any hurry to set up and fish unless, of course,
I saw fish crashing out in a spot I could get a rod to without
spooking them. That period from Saturday morning to late
afternoon may see very little from me in the way of wetting
a line but I'd be looking in as many nooks and crannies as
I could, climbing trees and trying to put myself where the
carp are likely to be when they are under pressure.

The swim became free and I quickly moved into it and started to change my end tackle for maximum effect.

Saturday Night

If you can only get one night in and can choose, forget Friday and go for Saturday. As long as you are not eating into the time you have to fish I'd try and get there mid-morning on Saturday to do all that I detailed earlier. It's not rocket science but look and find and you can catch. It may be that the pressure has reduced the visual signs of the fish, so a lot of your location will be based on educated guess work. That is not just going into an old favourite swim, but weighing everything up and giving it your best shot.

Saturday Night/Sunday Morning

If you are limited to a day session then the advice I gave about coming down during the early hours rings true for Sunday morning. Get yourself to the lake after midnight and look and listen for signs. As with Friday night, if carp are going to show it will more than likely be during the midnight to 4.00 a.m. period. One thing I have noticed on most waters I have fished is that the majority of anglers who fish Friday and Saturday nights, or just Saturday, are usually packed up by 11.00 a.m., unless it is a red letter day. Whether it's getting home to the family or the sport which tends to start early afternoon, if anglers are leaving

I hung on even as the
water was starting to
freeze and anglers
were leaving. I am
glad I did.

then that's when they go. So even if you can't get down in the middle of the night and have to arrive at a more respectable time then I wouldn't panic if it was still busy first thing. Sit on your hands, be prepared to drop into a swim if it's the right one and comes free. Come mid-afternoon on many waters you will have it to yourself.

Sunday Night

If you can pick any of the three nights this is the one, even at the expense of packing up in the dark and going straight to work from the lake. There will be nothing like the pressure there was on Friday and Saturday and believe me, the carp will know that. Lack of lines and noise must be obvious to them and if you can be stealthy in your approach you really can have some bumper catches, but for the weekend angler who can fish Sunday night it is a must. Even if you don't catch the peace alone is worth it!

Dawn to Dusk

Many day ticket waters have restricted hours and some allow no night fishing at all. On such venues it sounds obvious, but every minute counts. As I said previously, I want to be first in the queue and last out of the gate. Whatever it takes to be there first and stay there until the death you just do it. If you are a weekend angler even a few minutes either way can be the fine line between success and failure.

Whatever time you can find to fish at weekends there are many things you can do to increase your chances of success. I guarantee that if you follow the advice contained throughout this book you will catch, and be it stalking, or learning to get a bait on the money time and time again, the better you are at it, the more likely it will be you facing the camera. Carp are not impossible to catch at weekends, they just tolerate mistakes less and demand more from you as an angler. There are, however, certain things that years of experience have taught me to do to swing the odds my way so have a look at the points which follow and see if you can apply them. Consider how many of these points other anglers apply to their fishing. You can learn and benefit as much from what they don't do as well as what you can do.

Mobility

Many weekend anglers are naturally social anglers, which
I wouldn't criticise but you certainly can make that work
in your favour. If they are there to socialise with bivvy, gas
bottle , DVD player etc., what do you think are the chances
of them moving if they are in the wrong spot? What do you
think are the chances of them staying up until the middle
of the night looking for fish? Sometimes, the more anglers
I see with the best gear, the more confident I feel that my
minimalist approach will serve me well. Fish off the barrow
as much as you can and if your time is limited no amount
of hardship is too much, surely? So what if you move twice?
So what if you have to face the elements? So what if your
gear won't win awards? It's the carp not the pose that
matters. Often I have hung on to the death, moved when
a swim came free that I wanted, put a bait on a spot the
departing angler hadn't noticed, or covered, and had one.
It only requires that bait to be in the right place at the right
time to produce a take.

When the pressure is on, everything, and I mean everything, has to be right. Nothing is too much effort. I use these coloured marker pens to break up the profile of my hooklength.

Leave the Baits Out

Many weekend anglers tend to cast and recast far too
often and a newly positioned bait and strong-smelling
brand-new hookbait will often be viewed with suspicion
by pressured carp. Once I am sure a bait is on the right spot

I will leave it there till I go. That tactic alone has caught me a lot of weekend carp, but you really do need to be able to sit on those casting hands. When I even start to think about moving a bait I ask myself why. Why move it unless there is a good logical reason? There isn't one? Well don't do it. This particularly works well when margin fishing: a single bait lowered into the margins with no free offerings at all will be viewed without suspicion. It takes a lot of self belief to do this on a weekend but it works, I promise.

Don't be Drawn

Watch one angler wind in, recast and bait up and you will see other anglers follow his lead. It's almost as though it triggers some primeval urge to copy. This tends to happen at about 8.00 a.m. and 6.00 p.m. on the waters I fish – the first cast of the morning and last of the night. Even if you want to recast try doing it a lot earlier… or later. On one water I fish, on very short sessions, if I have not had a fish in the dark but feel carp are about, I will use the lightest lead possible and cast a bright pop-up out to the spots. Time and time again this works.

Energy

Your time will be limited at the weekend and it's important you give it everything you've got. No matter how big an eater you are, no matter how much you like your sleep, your energy and motivation are what will give you the edge over others. The more driven you are and the more lethargic they are, the better it is for you. I will eat and drink the bare minimum, but make sure I have enough fluid as I want to be on top of my game for the time I have. You are what you eat, and if you eat a lot and have a few alcoholic drinks, you will not be on top of your game. Watch the lads fish the BYCAC and because they only have twelve hours or so to qualify they exist on Red Bull and adrenaline – because it matters. Does it matter to you? I hope so!

Bait

The key to weekends on even 'supposedly' prolific waters is that less is more. Fish for one carp at a time because in all likelihood those carp will have had all manner of bait thrown at them from Friday night onwards. Simply piling it in will not improve your chances so concentrate on the hookbait and forget about the bait in the swim. You may be fishing over other people's bait so make that hookbait as appealing as possible and presented as well as possible.

Attitude

The biggest thing to get right at weekends is your attitude. If you turn up thinking you haven't got a chance because it's a weekend then you are not doing yourself any favours at all. In reality it's simply another day where the swim choice may be limited and carp more wary than usual. If your approach is 'I can and will succeed' then it's more likely that your efforts will be 100% and nothing will be too much trouble. The greatest thing about weekends is that they will improve your short session angling tremendously. If you can catch under pressure on limited time just imagine how many you will catch when the pressure is off! Sooner or later it will drop, and then the lessons you learnt from Friday through to Sunday will be more than worth it.

The water was packed, and I had to drop in between two other anglers. A bait in the edge on a slack line produced this bonus fish for me.

Chapter Seventeen
Multiple Hits:
When One Just Isn't Enough

How does twenty carp a year sound? Not bad, eh! How does sixty carp a year sound? A lot better, eh! Believe me that could be you. That is the difference between catching one each session and then getting your approach sorted and having three a session. When I look back at my records and diaries the years that I have done best on waters have been when I have really got into the flow of things, found out how to capitalise on opportunities that present themselves, and had multiple catches. Sure there have been times when I have had just one fish, or a blank, but when I've got it together you don't need to have many multiple catches to amass a 'best ever' season total.

It would be easy to think this only applies on prolific doubles waters but you are so wrong. Once you are in the zone whether that carp is 15lb or 25lb you can get multiple hits if numbers of fish of that size are present. The first time I recognised this was possible for big fish was way back in the early 90s doing overnighters on a local syndicate lake. The fish were shutting down at weekends but get it right midweek and even on a 12-hour overnighter you could have tremendous action. Four twenties, a thirty and a double in one night – fantastic! Even now on more pressured waters if you get it right, and, most importantly, are organised enough to take full advantage of the situation, you can have the big hits.

If you go with the attitude that you'd be lucky to catch just one you will never do it, as not only won't you fish as effectively as you need to, but you probably won't be able to take advantage of that window of opportunity, either. Daft really. Anyone can catch the odd one now and again but on short sessions when you really get it together, anyone can have the multiple catches you read about. Positive Mental Attitude: you have got to believe it can

happen to you, even on short sessions.

It just felt right.
Adjusting the buzzers
and believing that I
was going to have a
multiple hit.

The key to multiple catches is self belief and organisation but at the very start I must emphasise that you should set out to catch a carp, and if the opportunity presents itself then tailor your approach to catching more than one. Remember this is short session fishing and although firing out a big bed of bait may well work on longer sessions, I promise you that more often than not that approach will work against you on short sessions. The key to consistency is to be able to always be in with a good chance of at least one fish but when that opportunity avails itself take advantage of it. Even on waters I know well and would expect to catch a number of fish from, I know that carp don't always behave as expected, so I make sure that even if I have got it slightly wrong I am going to be in with a chance of at least one take. It may be that occasionally it will cost me a big hit but generally that's not the case. With that fish under my belt I may want to step up my bait but I can easily do that. If I have filled it in, or stuck myself in a no win situation swim-wise, its going to be a lot harder, if not impossible. As I said in the bait chapter most anglers fishing short sessions put too much bait in and apply it badly. Fish for single opportunities and as your experience grows you can apply some logical thinking to your approach and milk it on the red letter days.

Organisation is the key so come what may I do not turn up at a water without being prepared tackle wise and mentally disciplined to have that multiple catch. Here are a few of the 'musts' that you really need to look at.

Rigs

Although you should not pre-decide what rigs you are going to use it is plain daft not to have at least some 'starting' points with you. Obviously if it's a first trip or you have little experience that's more difficult but at that stage you'd hardly be looking at a multiple catch, would you? Multiple catches are when you get into the rhythm of a water and once you do then you find a way of making it happen. I have a number of Korda Rig Safes with me, five in fact, holding multi-rigs, stiff rigs and so on which means when I get to the water I have at least half a dozen of every rig I might need already tied. If I was fishing longer sessions then yes, maybe I would tie more up on the bank, but bank time is reserved for looking, moving and catching on short sessions. I make the time at home to ensure I have the presentations tied because that is part of being a successful short session angler. Whether I am watching television or just sitting in the kitchen I will make the time to ensure that the presentations are ready for the coming session. When I get there and choose the right rig to match the circumstances I tend not to tie anymore. With usually only 12 to 18 hours to play with it's not good use of my time. What I do have is the components to tie the rigs with

The Korda Rig Safe collection... coming to a lake near you soon.

me so that if the worst comes to the worst I can tie more up when I run out.

Being in a position to use a fresh rig after each fish with a needle-sharp hook can swing the percentages your way. I have seen people just keep using the same old hooks and wondering why it does not happen. Rigs are not just the hook and hooklength side of things: I also have spare leaders, leadcore and tubing end tackles tied up. If I need to change my end tackle I simply use one of the pre-tied ones I keep in a box inside my Fox Box. When the carp are really having it the last thing I want to do is be looping leadcore, threading beads and pegging safety beads – and neither do you !

Bait

The trick with bait is to fish for a carp at a time but if you are on them in numbers apply just enough feed to maximise the potential of the swim. Although I don't tend to use a lot of bait when I cast out – it's usually a PVA bag or stringer at most – I have plenty of bait with me. I tend to fish certain waters regularly and even if I only use a few baits during my fishing time I fire the rest out when I leave as prebaiting. Every bait without a hook in it should make the carp more confident in the long run, which can be very important when fishing regular short sessions. I am not prebaiting to get them 'locked' into my bait but as a way to maximise my chances next session. You can put more in if the opportunity avails itself whilst the rods are out, and if it doesn't you can still improve your chances for next time by putting it out as you leave. Now that's easier said than done because sometimes all you want to do is pack up and go home, right? Well look at the big picture and remember that short session success depends on long-term planning.

I started fishing stringers and was into them immediately.

Free offerings not attached to a hook are that long-term planning. I have yet to run out of bait on a 24-hour or less session – ever – so take more than you need even if you only use minimum whilst fishing. No matter how good you are multiple catches are not the norm so don't fall into the trap of having one or two big hits and then always going for a big hit with that same baiting approach. It will catch you out. One thing I do tend to do is have stringers already tied up, PVA bags loaded and so on. These additional bait delivery ideas mean that as soon as I wind in I can loop on that stringer or bag and get it straight out again. This is great when you get a cast wrong and lose the PVA bag: all you need to do is nick on a preloaded one and out it goes again. Sounds a minor thing but on red letter days it can save you so much time, and time is always against the short session angler so don't waste it.

I am always organised, and come what may, the camera gear is always set up.

Nets and Safety

Always take two landing nets. When you get one fish landed you should be leaving it in the net and putting that rod out again. This has caught me so many fish and yet I still see anglers making the same old mistakes. On average it can take anglers upwards of 20 minutes or more from landing a fish, weighing and photographing it before recasting. When I get one I ensure it is safe in the landing net, snip the trace and get that pre-tied end tackle back on the spot. It doesn't always work but it can never do any harm can it? If you want to photograph your fish the mat should already be down, and if you are on your own the camera on the tripod. Although I do fish with friends occasionally most of my fishing is done on my own. Once the rods are out, whether I feel confident or not, the

Multiple Hits: When One Just Isn't Enough

bank stick is set, the camera screwed onto the Gardner
Camera Angle and I'm ready for them. The chapter on
photography covers all this but if you really want to get the
most from your time the photographing of fish needs to be
done as quickly and efficiently as possible. There will be a
time to look back on the catch but when they are having it
every minute counts.

Spare Rod
If the water has a two rod limit I tend to have a spare
rod made up at all times. Not only does this mean that
I can get a rod out as soon as I have safely landed the
fish but I can also experiment with different end tackles
without having to break down one rod. On more prolific
waters when the action dries up I will tie up something
a little different, wind one in and cast out the new idea,
sometimes with immediate effect. It's also great just in case
you do have a crackoff or line damage and you can be
fishing immediately without having to respool. That is often
the difference between a fish or two... or many!

Setups
Although you should always have your lines marked and
sight lines drawn, if you want to have a multiple catch
you've got to do that. Only when you get everything right
will you get the maximum from your swim. That means
not making mistakes, be it not dropping spot on, forgetting
to add more feed and so on. The more right everything is
the better your results will be. Anglers who fish slapdash
are unlikely to have multiple hits. Anglers who get it right
and perform like fishing machines do. Watch anglers like
two-times British Carp Champions Bryan Jarrett and Dave
Gawthorn in action and you will see just how much hard
work and preparation goes into their setups. Nothing is
left to chance, from the way they position their rods, to
the way they spod or cast, ensuring maximum results on
minimum time.

Adapt
Sometimes to get the maximum from a swim you can't just
keep flogging to death the tactics that caught your last fish.
If you can adapt to changing conditions you are far more
likely to have more than one fish at a sitting. Maybe at the
start of the day your chances are best on the bottom but as

One from a huge winter
hit when conditions
were nothing special
but it all fell into place.

Multiple Hits: When One Just Isn't Enough

the sun creeps up it could be surface baits and Zig Rigs that are better? The more experienced you are as an angler the quicker you will pick up on this and be able to ring the changes to get the chances. I know it is tempting to keep doing the same old things but if you really want a multiple hit on a short session you need to be impatient. Don't rush things, but if it's not happening and you think it should be and think the change will help then do it. With two or three rods what have you got to lose?

Probably the biggest test of anybody who wants to have a multiple catch is the sheer physical and mental drive you need. Catching one or two in a session is great but once the numbers creep up it really does take effort. Effort is easy to write about but for many hard to find. I know when I have really had my red letter days I have had to push myself and keep telling myself that I need to take advantage of the occasion. I know it won't be a regular occurrence and I can look back at sessions when I know that with a little more effort I could, and should have, caught more carp. It is just as likely to happen in the winter as the summer so always be prepared come what may. Indeed in the colder months when angler pressure decreases and the carp start to shoal in preferred winter areas you really can have some big hits. I've had 22 January doubles in a day from one water when I got everything right. Think it was easy? Well the same water produced a blank weekend for me a month earlier when I got it very wrong. My carping conscience will not allow me to fish half-cocked, which can be both a good and a bad thing. It's bad in that I struggle to relax sometimes but it's good in that it makes me try my best or I'll feel annoyed with myself. 'Cundiff's Carping Conscience' will be the death of me one day! If you want maximum results you need to put in maximum effort, both in your preparation and attention to detail beforehand, and in your efforts on the bank. If I can do it I know you can so start working out how to turn one into two – or more!

Chapter Eighteen
Winter: Belief Is The Key

The best thing about winter carp fishing for the short session angler is that many anglers who fish for carp in the spring and summer don't bother in winter. Sure there are plenty of anglers who do fish for carp in the winter but from what I've seen there's a huge drop off. That's fantastic. The carp may be harder to catch, the conditions less favourable but the lack of other anglers means that it truly is you versus the carp. No searching for your sixth choice of swim, seeing the water being thrashed to a foam and dealing with World War 2 – heaven. No matter how hard the summer has been and dealing with angler pressure has done your head in, now is the time to get your head sorted, your carp brain on and be out there and catching.

Venue

Whilst it is possible to fish a number of venues ideally you should try to stick to one during the colder months. Winter carp are not easy to catch and unless you start to get a feel for the venue it really can be hard to get on top of it. When I look back at my successful winters it's not been one type of water which has shone, but the fact that I have fished a water hard from October through to March. Flitting here and there has ruined many a winter for me and even now, with all my experience, I still struggle on one-off trips to waters I don't understand.

The type of venue really depends on what you want from your carp fishing of course. Usually I spend the summer months targeting my big fish and in the winter I simply want somewhere I have a chance of action most sessions. The last thing I want to do is kill myself all winter for minimal rewards and then have spring and summer to grind through, too. A lot of very well-known carp anglers don't fish for carp in the winter simply because the size of

First light on an open pit. The water is starting to freeze up.

fish they wish to catch don't get caught regularly in the colder months. If these names avoid the harder big fish waters in the cold, then unless you feel you have a real edge which may work, it wouldn't be the type of water I'd expect you to target. Look for one with plenty of fish and hopefully not a lot of natural food. Although it sounds cruel the more they rely on anglers' baits the more likely they are to pick your bait up because they have to. And the more carp there are in the water the more they have to compete with each other. Shallow waters are best in that other than the problems with freezing up, they warm up and turn on a lot quicker and any sun or warmth will hopefully have the carp moving about. Less weed is better as the carp will have less natural food to feed on. Smaller acreage is better than bigger in that they are less likely to be out of range and therefore easier to find. Find them and you are a long way towards catching them.

Planning

Getting it wrong in summer is bad enough, but getting it wrong in winter can be disastrous. Weather conditions will generally be worse so be aware how long it will take you to get there and plan alternative routes to use if a road is closed. What is it like getting there in the snow and ice?

How soon does it freeze? Who can you contact to find out if it is frozen? A lot of your fishing is probably going to be carried out in the day so it's important to be there just before first light: if you don't know how long it takes to get there you may miss out on the dawn spell. Simple mistakes will cost you dearly and those mistakes are generally unnecessary!

Whatever you do visit it at least once before your campaign really starts and don't leave your winter fishing too late. For some anglers winter carp fishing is December onwards but if your first trip is in December you may be playing catch-up all winter long. Personally, unless I am still pursuing target fish on a local water I would not want to start a winter campaign any later than the start of November, and preferably the middle of October onwards. That way you will be able to find out how the carp have behaved late summer/early autumn and hopefully not waste too much of your limited winter time building up that picture. You are more likely to see carp in the September/October period, too, and if you can catch one or two to get your winter campaign off to a good start it's a great confidence builder.

Timing

Although in the summer months you can turn up day or night and hopefully find and catch fish on many winter waters that just isn't possible. Although the fish will feed, their need to feed will decrease. Feeding spells reduce and unless you are there at the right time a miss is as good as a mile. The more time you can spend at the water the better, which may contradict some advice on winter fishing that I have seen. Finding these 'mythical' feeding spells and just popping down for an hour or two is all well and good when the water is very close but if it isn't it's impossible.

Yes, I have found certain times that are better for action than others but I have yet to find a water where, during a winter campaign, I could only get a bite at a certain time

The key is to keep watching and waiting. I was, I did, and I caught.

and the rest of the time was wasted. I try to spend at least 10 hours fishing when doing days which means, if allowed, an hour before dark and an hour or two into dark.

Occasionally I will fish a water where it just isn't possible to do day sessions so I fish for 24 hours at least every fortnight. Personally, I'd try to fish 24 hours once a week then 48 hours every alternate week if you can. The more you fish the more you will identify the better periods, but until you do, even the short session carper will have to put in the groundwork. When I find these periods I will do all it takes to reap the rewards. So if it's first light for takes my baits will be in place well before first light. If it's at dusk then I fish well into dark.

I see many anglers turn up an hour too late and leave an hour too early!

Location

The advice I read when Tim Paisley wrote 'they are where they are and that's where you fish' is spot on for short session carpers. All waters are different and what works on one water in the cold may not work on another. I know some waters where it seems you can only get a take fishing over dead weed, yet on another it's in clear open water where the carp seem to like to lay up. As many of you will be new to carp fishing a little more guidance would be helpful on this aspect, and there are some factors that seem to be consistent across a broad spectrum of venues.

A Fish do show less in the cold so if you see one that's often as good as it gets so cast to it or move to it. The carp will not come to you as they may do in summer.

B The more you look the easier it is to find them. Leave your books and DVD player at home and watch the water like a hawk. Just spotting one fish could mark a winter holding area which you can exploit.

C Never neglect the shallows. I have seen carp in water only just deep enough to cover them so keep looking.

D If you can't find them the middle is as good as anywhere and I don't say that flippantly. On a number of waters the carp do favour the middle in the winter and if you can ascertain the depth they are at you can reap the rewards.

Winter: Belief Is The Key

E Location is not just where the fish are in front of you but also what depth they are at, so be prepared to experiment with the depth of your bait.

F If the water has islands of any type try to find the spots which are sheltered from the cold winter winds. Carp use these to lay up in for obvious reasons.

G If you can find spots that receive most of the sunlight and are sheltered so will the carp, these areas are always worth trying unless you know the fish are elsewhere.

I can't reiterate how important location is and if this book teaches you one thing as a short session carper it's that if you want to be successful your eyes are for watching the water, not watching DVDs.

Tackle

Generally I fish shorter sessions and until I feel I know where the fish are I will be very mobile in my approach, simply fishing off the barrow. I would never go without a shelter of some type and often fish under it unless it is very settled weather. Setting up a brolly takes under a minute but the shelter it gives you is more than worth it. Don't be too comfortable as having a mid-afternoon nap is not going to help you locate the fish is it? As long as the tackle allows me to get to the fish then what I use in winter is not too dissimilar to what I use in summer, I just take less of it!

Bait and Baiting

In a word – minimal. If I was fishing a local water regularly then I would keep a bait like Nutrabaits Trigga Ice ATS or Nutrabaits Enervite Gold going in. However, if not I would not feel too much of a disadvantage taking minimal feed with me. Unless I knew different it would always only be stringers, PVA bags or singles. Occasionally I will scatter a few around so that the carp do find the odd one or two. However, no amount of bait will get them to feed in the cold if they are not that way inclined. All you are doing is cutting down on your chances. As I leave I'd certainly stick out bait so that they find plenty for the next time I come but not in an attempt to get them to feed more. Winter carp do seem to change their preferences very quickly. One day it may well be a Pineapple bottom bait but the next day it

may have to be a darker feed bait. If I felt I was on fish and was not getting a take within the hour I'd ring the changes to try to get a take. You have nothing to lose so be prepared to try all you have with you.

Maggots can be deadly if you don't have a huge silver fish problem but they are not always the answer on all waters and the nuisance fish can drive you crazy. Ball Pellets are a great advantage to get feed in and for the carp to hear bait plopping in but nothing to fill them up with. Remember you are looking for that all important first bite each time so less is more most of the time. Sit on your hands and you won't go too far wrong.

Top When the water is deathly cold, a bit mix with maggots is a good option.

A single hookbait did the trick with this mid-winter mirror.

Rigs

The finer the better. Once the natural food dies back and the fish stop moving around the water will clear and end tackles can look oh so crude if not sensibly thought out. An end tackle which blends in will not cost you any fish but it may well catch you bonus fish. If the water allows it then a size 12 will get you more bites than a size 10 and so on. Any mistakes you make with your rigs in the colder months will be magnified greatly so don't make any. The sharpest hooks, the finest of braids and properly thought out PVA setups. Carp will not tolerate mistakes and neither should you. Not all takes will be screamers so if you can fish running leads and set your lines up to watch for gentle takes then do so. Lethargic and clued-up carp will do you in the blink of an eye.

Tips and Tactics

The hardest part about being a short session carper in the colder months is not the time but the self belief. You need to really believe they are catchable and that you are the one to catch them. The best tip I can give you is to go as often as possible and give it 100%. You will inevitably be fishing less than you do in summer so increase your efforts. No matter how cold it is they can be caught if you have got

your tactics sorted. Multiple catches are possible and if you can catch one through logical thinking you can catch a lot more. The first one is often the hardest but if you caught it by means of a measured approach it shouldn't be too hard to take full advantage. You need to keep an open mind at all times. Be it a Zig Rig on a freezing cold day or floaters in a sheltered spot when the sun's out, don't be a slave to the standard bright pop-up method.

What a cracker! Single bait at range was the key to success that day.

Winter carp fishing is your chance to have the water to yourself on many occasions. Get it right and the multiple catches you couldn't achieve in the summer months may come your way. But you've got to be there because you won't catch them from your armchair!

Chapter Nineteen
Safety Matters

Although this book is aimed at helping you catch carp on short sessions I think that any book aimed at helping anglers catch carp should also help anglers look after the carp they land. Whether you fish for one hour or one week, the attention you give the fish and the thoughts you apply to safety should be no different. Inevitably short session see you do everything at a quicker pace than longer sessions but the carp's safety should never be compromised by this pace. Whilst I know there are people who truly do all they can to look after their carp there are many anglers, who through ignorance or just plain laziness, don't. Hopefully the advice I am going to give you here will help you help anglers who are not as safety minded as they should be. Whilst I am never one to tell anglers what to do, when it comes to the safety of the carp you really do have to speak up at times whether you want to or not. No syndicate leader or day ticket manager would ever criticise you for that, I am sure.

There has been much written about looking after carp and in a book this size I am limited to what I can put in so please look at the additional reading in the reference chapter. Carp safety falls into two main areas when it comes to short session angling. The safety of the carp before you land it and then the safety of the carp when it's in the net, and afterwards.

Carp Safety Before Netting

Although locating carp is often one of the main keys to success, especially on shorter sessions, locating them is one thing, landing them another. Think of where you have found them or want to fish. What chance do you have of landing the fish? If the water is weedy or snaggy you really must be realistic as fishing for chances is both pointless for you and potentially dangerous to the carp. Unless I am totally convinced that I have a realistic chance of landing every fish I hook I simply won't set up in that swim. Although merely fishing for carp gives me enough of a buzz, if I am going to put in all that effort to hook one I want it in my net and recorded on camera.

Be honest with yourself, if you hook a carp are you going to be able to land it? Is there a better swim to fish the same area? If you can present a bait and hook the carp, what is there between you and the fish? Banks of weed, gravel bars and the like can cut you off, weed you up and cause untold damage to a fish so please use your carp brain not just to hook them but to be in a with a chance of landing them. There is a great temptation, especially when you are inexperienced or struggling, to fish as close as possible to snags or weed to fish for chances and this really is not acceptable. Carp are prone to causing themselves terrible damage if they get snagged up and although that can happen even to the best of us, the closer you fish and the more chances you take, the more likely it is to happen. Remember you are fishing for the picture not the take so before you cast out be honest. Am I going to be able to get to my rods and get the carp under control or will it be solid.... and inevitably lost and damaged? If you've taken the time to purchase this book and read this chapter I am sure you won't fish for chances but be caring in your approach.

Think of the tackle you are using, too. Is it strong enough to land the carp where you hook it? Most rods and reels are fine but the line on some anglers' reels is poor. It needs to be strong enough to control the fish you hook and maintained well enough so that it does not lose its strength. Properly loaded line continuously checked and discarded when necessary is the only answer. If there is weed about 15lb main line is a must. Lead systems need to be able to discharge leads when required and the hook and hooklength

Top If you are fishing in weed go for a lead clip which discharges the lead when necessary.

Fishing tight to snags and weed means not only must you take care where to cast but be sure that your tackle won't let you down. The Basia clutch has never let me down.

combination must not cause damage to the flank or mouth of the fish. Whatever leadcore or leader setup you use it should be as safe as you can make it. Nothing is 100% safe as you are casting into an environment that is not in any way similar to your kitchen table. All you can do is your best. Even on a short session before I cast out I will always set up at least one landing net. Think I am stating the obvious? You'd be surprised at how many people I have seen playing a carp whilst trying to set up a net! And similarly you must never dismantle your net until all the rods have been wound in.

Before I cast out I always have my unhooking mat to hand and although it may not be positioned in the ideal place for photography I know where it is if I need it. As well as the largest mat you can afford and can carry you must also have a pair of forceps for unhooking the fish, a pair of cutters in case you need to snip a hook in half, and some antiseptic carp care gel as marketed by Kryston or Nash. Always ensure that your landing net mesh is assembled the right way as some nets have clips on them to clip onto the handle. If you were to lift a carp up in the net and the

Sitting on the rods as the end tackles are tight to the pads.

clip was between it and the mesh it can mark or damage the fish. When you are fishing and using audible indicators ensure they are on. Waking up the next morning to find a carp weeded up is stupid and irresponsible. If a carp hooks itself you must know you are to be able to take immediate action. Although I do see it advocated, when packing the buzzers away and leaving the rods on the ground you must be very careful. If your clutch is set firm and the carp runs the rod may well be dragged in. It happened to me once and I had to swim to the lilies as luckily the rod was sticking up like Excalibur to show me where it was! I landed that carp but it was a lesson to me to not do that again, or to always leave the clutches free running if I really want to leave them out till last thing.

Many of the buzzers that we use nowadays have remote sounder units which enable you to hear your alarm even when the buzzer head is turned down. They are not designed to allow anglers to meet in one communal swim for a social and use the remote to warn of a take from somewhere else on the lake. Leaving your rods not only breaks Environment Agency rules and many fishery byelaws but on more and more waters is likely to get you

A distinctive mirror when I needed to have all my wits about me to hit, hold and land.

banned by the bailiff. Use the remote so you don't need to have your buzzers on full volume, not so you can leave your rods out whilst you are away from the swim. This is an important element of fish safety in terms of avoiding getting fish snagged. If you want a social wind in and enjoy it without putting the carp at risk.

Carp Safety When Netted

Once I have cast out unless I am roving about I always set up my camera equipment next, which means the mat, unhooking gear and water bottle are in place. This is all covered in the photography chapter and goes hand in hand with safety. When I hook a carp I want it photographed and back in the water as soon as possible; combining its safety and getting a good picture without compromising either. Here are a few pointers that to me are an absolute must when it comes to netting carp.

As soon as you net the fish be very careful before you drag the landing net to the bank. You should envelop the fish in the net but not pull it in to check the size of the fish. The closer in to the bank it is the more likely you are to encounter stanchions, broken bits of trees, boulders and shallower water, etc. Bouncing a carp in on these can be very dangerous. Carefully pull the handle back and see what you have landed.

If you are using two nets as I recommend, then in all likelihood the netted carp will be to the left or right of your setup. Put the handle down and then peg the net down with a standard T-peg which you would use for your bivvy. This will prevent the carp from surging away with the net whilst you are getting things ready. It may be that you are going to cast another rod to the spot but ensure that netted carp is going nowhere.

Although you can unhook a carp whilst it is still in the net I do not advocate it. Wiggling a hook about can cause damage to the carp's mouth and I have seen a carp thrash and transfer a hook from its mouth to a finger in the blink of the eye. Believe me the anglers concerned never tried that again. If I am on my own I tend to simply cut the hooklength an inch or so from the hook and leave the carp in the net. This frees up the rod which means you are less likely to stand on it, catch it in the bushes or end up dragging the carp on the ground whilst struggling with rod and net.

Safety Matters

With your rod out of the way ensure that all
is ready for the pictures of the carp if you intend to
photograph it. If you are on your own then the camera
needs to be ready, the remote to hand and the unhooking
kit next to the mat. If someone else is doing your pictures
ensure they know what to do before you hold the fish up.
Trying to show them how to use your camera and hold the
fish at the same time is a recipe for disaster.

If you are going to weigh the fish ask yourself do
you really need to? For some it is important for others not
so. Personally speaking I do not weigh carp which are
obviously under twenty pounds simply because I have
caught enough fish not to bother with lists, but I am able to
appreciate the carp for what it is, not necessarily its weight.
If it's around 20lb or more I may well weigh it so that when
I do write about it I am exact. For whatever reason I feel
comfortable describing a fish as a double without weighing
it, but not comfortable describing a fish as a twenty without
weighing it. But that's me and you must choose what's best
for you without putting the carp at risk.

Before I lift the carp out of the water I ensure
that its fins are not bent back and there are no twigs or
sticks trapped in the mesh which could damage the fish.
Carefully the carp is taken to the mat usually by me
breaking down the arms of the landing net and carrying
the frame and net to the mat. Trying to hold a net handle
and a carp at the same time is dangerous so try not
to do it.

Once the fish is on the mat I use forceps to take the
hook out and that hook goes in my little bucket that holds
all my unhooking paraphernalia. The hookhold is treated
with gel and then I take the photographs.

It really would be possible to write a book about
carp safety but a lot of it is down to commonsense,
preparation and simply caring enough. On your shorter
sessions you are trying to make every minute count so the
better prepared you are the less you have to fiddle around
with the carp, and the sooner it is back in the water –
the sooner you will have another one!

Chapter Twenty
Picture Time: Smile Please

arp fishing is different things to different people but generally most carp anglers have one thing in common: whatever carp we catch it is nice to have a good photographic record of it. I have been carp fishing for many years but even today once a carp is a double or bigger I try to take at least a picture of each side of it to relive that moment. When you are short session fishing things naturally are more rushed and in the rush to get the fish photographed, safely back to the water and a rod in position again it can be easy to not have the time to appreciate your catch. Having a good picture of the fish helps you relive your memories and I think it sometimes justifies all the effort we put in towards the catching of our quarry. I tend to spend as much effort as possible getting my pictures right, not only for me but because it is important when writing for publications to show the fruits of my labour and advice. From a bog-standard 110 camera in 1979 to now taking two digital cameras I have seen many changes, made many mistakes and I'm sure that if you follow the advice I am about to give you won't have to suffer the frustrations I have been through. All it takes is a little time, some cost and, as usual for the short session carp angler, being organised.

When it comes to taking good quality pictures there are two scenarios to consider. One is when someone else takes your pictures and the second is when you do them on your own. Unless you always go fishing with a friend no matter how much you get the first one right you must be in a position to get the second one right, too. Big fish and red letter days can come along when you least expect them: that fish and that day may never happen again so there is no room for getting things wrong. You can't go back if you don't get it right.

Picture Time: Smile Please

The Equipment

Digital Camera

Without doubt if you take your fishing seriously you need to invest in a digital camera. Whilst a standard camera using print or slide film will take great pictures it has one main drawback, you will not be able to see the results until you develop the film the next day or next week. Imagine catching the fish you have dreamt of and then your friend or you have cut its tail off in the pictures. That has happened many times, and to the best of us. With digital cameras you can check the image you have captured instantly. Is it focused, light enough and all in the picture? If not you can adjust and get it right in seconds. You can pick up a good digital camera for well under £100 and that investment can last you... well years and years. Compared to what you spend on bait, petrol, rods and reels it will be nothing but skimp and you will regret it one day. I don't intend this to be a lesson on which camera to use or not to use so all I will do is tell you what I use and why.

I have two digital cameras:

Canon 350D SLR This is my trophy shot camera as it has an infrared remote that means once it is on my bankstick I simply point the tiny infrared clicker at it, squeeze it and it focuses and takes the pictures brilliantly. You can pick these up brand new for around £250 and second-hand from very reputable camera shops at around half that price, usually with a warranty. All my self takes are with this camera.

Compact or SLR.
You decide?

Panasonic Lumix FS62D Compact This is the one I hand to anyone I want to take a picture of me with a fish. A large screen makes it a lot easier for them not to miss anything and as it's typical of most digital compacts, it is probably similar to what they may have themselves. It does not have an infrared remote so cannot be used for self takes. Cost is just under £100 but again, second-hand, you can pick up an immaculate one for half the price.

If you can only afford one it must be a camera that can be used with an infrared remote. Not all can so ensure that yours can, or get one that does. Providing you look after them they should last you for years. My Canon is well over five years old and although I use my Lumix on a daily basis I would expect that to last at least as long.

Infrared Remote Absolutely essential if you want to take self-take pictures. Not all cameras are compatible with these remotes so be careful before you buy that 'bargain'. I place my infrared in a clear hook packet and seal it with Sellotape so that water does not get inside it and corrode it internally. These only cost around £10 and are an essential camera accessory.

Spare Batteries and Cards You can't be too prepared if you are a short session carper. Although I always charge my camera batteries regularly I do have a spare one with me for the

Top **My little box of spares which has everything from remotes to Camera Angles, batteries to camera cards.**

Keep the lens clean and your pictures will come out much better.

Canon. I also have a spare camera card for the Canon just in case I have a big hit on a prolific water. I probably take far too many pictures of each fish but back at home I can delete them to leave only the best for my use but be careful as multiple shots can eat up your available images on the bank.

Cleaning Kits and Suchlike I keep both cameras in a Fox Evolution Camera bag which also houses a box of spares as I detailed above. I have a very basic cleaning kit for the cameras and everything is kept in heavy-duty clear plastic bags for protection from moisture.

Self-Take Gear As well as the infrared remote I have a very sturdy bankstick and a Gardner Camera Angle to allow me to position my Canon perfectly. Although some people take tripods I use a screw in Steade's bankstick.

Picture Time: Smile Please

This I have coated in fluorescent tape so I can see it at night. When screwed into the ground it is more stable than any tripod I have seen and, importantly, can't be moved or knocked over. Once in position you know all your pictures will be right as it is the Camera Angle that you use to line up the shot. Gardner's Camera Angle is a must-have item and once your camera is on it you can line things up perfectly. Easy to use, costs under £10 and is a must for every reader.

Pictures by Fellow Anglers Although this sounds easy once you know the basics of photography and have your self-take system perfected it is easier to do it yourself rather than leave it in the hands of another person, unless that person really knows what he is doing. For the purposes of this let's presume they do and you want your picture taking. Well before you lift the carp to the mat you need to get a few things sorted. Ensure your watch is off and if you have any neck chains they are tucked into your shirt and bracelets are taken off. These can scratch carp and easily rip a scale or two off. Think about what you are wearing.

The rods are out and the camera is in position for action. Within twelve hours I'd photographed six carp on my own and then set off to work.

How will the carp stand out against you? If it's a common or pale fish a dark shirt will show it off well, say black, green or blue. If it's a mirror or leather carp a brighter shirt is best, so red or grey for contrast works well. You must not wear anything with a buckle or zip on it as it will mark the carp so generally a T-shirt or sweatshirt is best.

Think about the background, too. If possible some kind of background is better than nothing behind you. You will look less stark, the flash, if necessary, will have something to bounce off and your picture will look a lot more impressive. Is the mat down and in position? Do you have a small bucket

Having the luxury of fishing with a friend occasionally means I can do the honours for him and vice versa... Brian Skoyles is the captor on this occasion.

of water to pour on the fish? Are your unhooking tools and weighing gear in position? Right, game on...

Get your potential photographer to kneel where you will be when holding the fish above the unhooking mat. Put yourself a reasonable distance from the fish and either get closer or further away as you look through the viewfinder. Imagine yourself in that shot. With you and carp in shot will there be plenty of space around the carp so he can't cut its head or tail off? Once you feel you are in position place the camera on a box or something similar and instruct the photographer as to where he takes the picture from and not to in anyway attempt to mess with the zoom. It is perfect as it is, tell him!

Go to the water and lift the carp out following the procedure I outlined in the carp safety chapter. Unhook the carp and treat the hook wound and weigh it, if necessary. Ensure your hands are wet at all times. With the carp on the unhooking mat pick any leaves or weed off it and gently pour water over it. Under no circumstances wipe the carp or you will remove the precious mucus that protects the fish.

Lift the carp up slightly off the mat and with the head angled slightly up and the carp slightly angled to the photographer ask him what he sees through the viewfinder. Is it all in with plenty or room all around you and the fish?

Picture Time: Smile Please

Watch what he is doing and try to be firm but to instill confidence in him. You can usually tell by the angle of the camera whether he is getting it right or not!

I usually put auto flash on my Lumix and with the carp slightly at an angle it stops the flash bouncing straight back and wiping out the definition of the fish. Get him to do at least six shots of each side. You can slightly alter your pose but it's important that he does not move. Make sure he stays kneeling or standing as you set the picture up in the first place. Keep the fish close to you and pour water on it yourself if need be. He must not move at all.

Once you've got the pictures taken get him to you to show you the images on digital playback. Usually I put the carp down on the mat, wipe my hands and then check them myself. All good? Right give him back the camera, return that carp and go get another one!

Sounds a long time? No, it should take under two minutes maximum.

Pictures by Self-Take Process This sounds the more complicated of the two methods but once you get into the swing of it I can honestly say I prefer it rather than leaving it in the hands of someone else. Practice makes perfect and if I – with my limited knowledge and interest in cameras – can do it, anyone can. First essential, of course, is to sort your background as I detailed earlier. If you are fishing into dark consider what the background will look like in the dark just as much as you would in the light. I usually look for a bush or tree and place my unhooking mat just in front of it allowing me to get between the bush and the mat.

With the rods safely in position and providing it is safe get the self-take gear set up immediately – yes, even before you have a coffee or a relax. You never know when that first take will come so get it done now so there is no panic later. Generally the place I am taking my pictures will be next to my shelter so I am no more than feet from my rods when I am doing all this. Unless you are fishing a very tight swim this should not be a problem.

Get your camera and screw the Gardner Camera Angle into it. Now get your bankstick and stand roughly six feet from the mat. This is about right for cameras with 18-55mm lenses, which most are. Kneel down around this area and with the camera switched on look through the viewfinder. How does it look? Need to be a little bit closer?

Maybe a bit further away? Just right? Great.

Now screw the Camera Angle into the inner of the bankstick and remove this inner part. Screw the outer body of the bankstick into the ground until it is rock solid. Usually this means I have pushed around three inches or more of the bankstick into the ground. Place the inner stick which has the Camera Angle and the camera on it into the outer body of the bankstick.

Get the Camera Angle and turn it at 45 degrees so that the camera is in a portrait not landscape position. Open the focus out fully and look through the viewfinder. I know that on the waters I fish the biggest carp I catch will never be longer than the width of my unhooking mat so if each side of the mat is in then the shot will be perfect. If not I move the mat back a little.

Think about where you will be kneeling on the mat and set your camera at the right height. The Steade's bankstick has a very heavy-duty tightening nut and once you do tighten it I can assure you it will not move. Switch the camera on and set it to self timer mode and flash on, too. Walk to the mat taking with you the infrared remote.

Kneel exactly where you would expect to kneel with the carp and pointing your infrared at the camera take a test shot. Check it on digital playback for positioning. Perfect? If not move the mat until it is. Most times I can do it in one shot but occasionally I have to move the mat a foot or so back. I can assure you that with practice you will be able to do that. Satisfied with that? Then put the lens cover on and switch the camera off. If the water I am fishing is secure I leave my camera on the stick, carefully place the soft bag over it, and on top of that I place another bag. This is actually the top off a dryer cover that I use to keep my rod sleeves from banging around in the car. It is a perfect fit and as it is heavy-duty, green and waterproof it keeps the camera dry and out of sight. If your water is not secure simply undo the tightening nut from the bank stick and place the camera attached to the Camera Angle and inner stick under your shelter for security.

When you get a fish at night it's simply a case of uncovering the camera and switching it on, or putting the inner stick back into place. Before you take the fish out of the water you might want to take another test shot just in case but in time you will realise that if you set it up correctly during the day it won't be any different at night. With your jacket off, your chain tucked away and the fish weighed, treated and wet hold it up, squeeze the infrared and try to look happy! I will take six or more shots of each side, slightly changing my angle and never holding the carp flat on, or fully upright, to avoid flash bounce.

Again, it sounds a lot of trouble to go to but I can assemble my self-take gear in under two minutes and the fish isn't out of the water any longer for a self-take than a picture taken by another angler. Organisation, preparation and practice will show you that. In a nutshell you can take pictures which are good enough to grace the cover of a magazine and are a worthy memory of the effort you have put in. I have not covered sacking of fish as I believe it unnecessary on 99% of occasions and is putting your desire for a daylight shot above the safety and health of the carp. That's my view: this is my book so take that how you want!

Chapter Twenty One
Alternative Baits To Buy A Bite

For many carp anglers 'the big secret' seems just out of reach. Be it a special water, magical bait, secret rig or approach, if they just had that missing link it would all fall into place. Sorry but that's rubbish. A long time ago when you could be first on a water, first on a new bait, or wonder rig, that may well have been true but for the majority of waters that you are going to target it's just not so. Carp fishing is a game of percentages and the more you get right the more likely you are to catch. Bait is just one part of the percentage game and its importance varies from water to water, day to day and from one angler to another. You can have a great bait and put it in the wrong place and it might as well be a poor bait! You can have a great applied food source like a boilie but put it on the bottom when all the carp are on the surface and what good is it going to do? However, when you have read and digested all I have written I am hoping you won't make those mistakes. Your approach will be the correct one and most important of all in terms of this chapter, your bait will be the right one for the right spot.

Throughout the book in the chapters I have written on each of the seasons and those on the stalking and floater fishing approach I have detailed the baits I have found to work. My first approach would always be those that I have detailed. However, carp are not always as kind to us as we want them to be and for a number of reasons sometimes you will have to step away from the standard approach and instead try to get a bite by tinkering with your bait or baiting. This 'buying a bite' using bait is really no different to 'buying a bite' through rigs or tactical approach. Sometimes a bait in open water will produce when normally a bait tight to the pads is the way to succeed. A 3-inch hooklength will produce when a 12-inch one always used to work. A running lead may fool them instead of a fixed lead, and so on. It's having an ability to recognise that something which should be happening, isn't happening, so let's try something to buy a bite.

So start with the basics that suit you and your approach best, but when something isn't happening and you want to step things up bait-wise, here are some ideas that get me a bite. This is not a comprehensive bait chapter but some proven ideas that work for me when my standard baiting approach doesn't seem to.

Tiger Nuts

In the summer months when even the best boilie seems to stutter I find that fishing tigers, albeit in small quantities, can be a real blank saver. Although they can work all year round I have found that on popular waters carp can become very wary, almost fed up of boilies in the summer months. Even if they do eat them it can be very hard for you to get them to make a mistake with the hookbait. The tiger nut is a winner at this time of year and has caught

Top By cubing your hookbait you make rejection of the bait a lot more difficult.

When everyone was on supple Hairs I used to continue the fluorocarbon for the Hair and it worked a treat well before the KD was published.

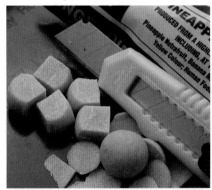

me a lot of bonus fish when all else fails. I don't prepare them myself but get a can of the brilliant Dynamite Baits version. They do Monster, Mini and Chopped and one can of each will last you all summer and catch you a lot of carp. In the cans they last years, but once opened their shelf life obviously lessens. What I do is open a can of each and pour them into heavy duty and correctly labelled freezer bags. They are then placed in the chest freezer. When I go fishing I simply place a small handful of each in a labelled mini hookbait pot and what I don't use gets thrown in when I leave. Fished on a Hair rig, even in isolation, they are wonderful. For stalking they really take some beating, too. On short sessions in very warm weather mixing the chopped tigers sparingly with groundbait, balling it in and fishing a tiger nut over the top is brilliant. The oil from the ground bait and chops draws

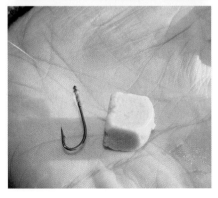

them in and the hookbait does the rest. Another simple little idea that works well is combining a tiger nut and a boilie. Although you can use a bottom bait I tend to combine a small pop-up with the tiger nut. Then, using a craft knife, I trim down the pop-up until the two of them just sink. Great in isolation or in a PVA bag of crumbed boilies and dried tiger nut chops.

Maggots

You'd have to be blind not to have seen the effect these have had on some waters in recent times. Maggots have always worked for carp but when they are applied by high-profile carp anglers on waters with big carp in them their use is brought to light. Carp love maggots but so do all sorts of other fish from eels to perch to bream. Great bait but non selective. In winter I will always try maggots, especially when the nuisance fish are minimal and the bottom is fairly hard. In summer maggots can simply be too attractive to everything else to give the short session carper a chance of success. If you are reeling in nuisance fish every couple of minutes you may not be doing your chances much good. However, for stalking they are brilliant and a bunch lowered to fish is often taken immediately. A great bait to have with you when times are hard but beware their attraction to everything that swims!

Worm and Boilie

Although the worm on its own is a great change-bait, when you combine it with a boiled bait it really comes into its own, especially for stalking fish. I tend to fish a pop-up as normal but use the worm threaded on the longshank hook to counterbalance the pop-up. The movement of the worm coupled with the visual impact of the boilie can prove too much for the carp to resist. Great when you can find and see the carp but, as with maggots, can be a little unselective at times.

Cubed and Trimmed Baits

Although the majority of boilies that are applied to waters are round you can really improve your chances by trimming and altering the shape of your hookbait. A round boilie – be it 10mm or 24mm – can easily be sucked in but it can just as easily be blown out. By trimming the edges with a craft knife you can change

A washed-out bait fooled this lovely common carp.

it to any shape you want. Not only does this make the hook more likely to waft around in the carp's mouth and take hold if ejection is attempted, but once you break the skin of the bait you are allowing the attractors to seep out easier. For short sessions this is ideal. A trimmed bait does not look as obvious as a bog-standard boilie. I have seen carp ignore round baits but sample the cubed ones almost immediately. Most of my hookbaits are trimmed and this has given me an edge on many waters.

Washed-Out Baits

Although the ingredients of a bait and the attractors which are in it can attract the carp to the bait, they can at times be too strong, or the carp can, by association, learn that the strongest smelling ones are to be avoided. For whatever reason on some waters carp do not appear to take baits until they have been in the water for some time. By soaking your hookbaits before you use them you can duplicate this effect of washing out the attractors. You must use water from the lake not tap water as the two will be completely different, believe me. On waters where you are sure the carp are eating the bait but not taking the hookbait, soaking baits is a great way to buy that bite in the limited time you have at the water. Obviously different baits vary in their 'hardness' so experiment to see how your bait

behaves when it is soaked for 4, 12 or however many hours.

Glugs and Soaks

The purpose of the hookbait is to get the carp to take that bait it into its mouth where the hook can take hold. Obviously to do this the carp needs to be able to locate your hookbait either by searching for it or you putting it where you know the carp are, or will be. By glugging a bait you are in effect 'amping' up the 'find me and eat me' signal, a tactic which can be very effective indeed. The colder the water is the more a bait's attractors will be locked in, so for winter fishing soaking your hookbaits in a glug is a great edge.

To get the glugs to really soak in warm them on your radiator (which sadly means you have to switch them on...).

Many companies do glugs to match their own range so check with the company that produces the bait you are using. One thing I do is trim all my hookbaits before I glug them. Trimmed hookbaits will draw in more of the glug which on short sessions is great for increasing leakage when cast out.

Alternative Hookbaits

It is very tempting when you are loose feeding or have applied a bait to use that same bait as a hookbait. Often this works but when times are hard and you need to buy a bite you may need to think out of the box. If I am using a dark coloured bait like Nutrabaits' Big Fix Mix or Biollix, by fishing an alternative bait over it the carp sometimes seem to take that quickly. A white or yellow bait is sometimes taken very soon after casting out. One tactic I had on a big fish water I tackled was to cast an alternative pop-up at dawn over my food baits that had been put in when I arrived at the lake the previous evening. Not only can you use a single alternative bait over your standard free offerings but you can combine an alternative bait with a standard bait 'Snowman style'. Or maybe an alternative bait such as a tiger nut over boilies. Remember you do not have the time to sit and wait so try to get that carp to have a go at the different hookbait.

Alternative Baits To Buy A Bite

Paste

I covered this variation in the bait delivery chapter but
if you want to increase the attraction levels around
your hookbait without adding more feed items, take
advantage of paste. Particularly good in cold weather
due to the leak-off rate it is also good in summer where
nuisance fish can be a problem. As they break off bits of
the paste more and more attractors will leak off, hopefully
drawing in your target fish.

Meat

When I first started carp fishing luncheon meat, along with
cheese, was seen as one of 'the' baits to use for carp, but
with the advent of the boilie it seemed to get forgotten
about – which makes it an ideal alternative bait for you
to try. Straight off the shelf Pepperami sticks are a brilliant
bait to have with you at all times and with the garlic and
fat in them are both potent and semi buoyant. Indeed the
new chilli version really packs a punch, ideal for when you
want that bite – and quick. Simply open the packaging,
cut a piece to match your hook size and either Hair rig it
or side hook it when stalking. With luncheon meat, either
the bog-standard one off the shelf or the more potent Van
Den Eynde work well and can be used straight from the tin.
Because luncheon meat is quite soft, unless you are fishing
it close in, I recommend gently frying it in a pan. Not only
does this make it more user-friendly and tougher for casting,
but if you fry it in a table spoon of spice from the local
supermarket its attraction level is increased too. You can do
that on the bankside and can even colour it for increased
visual appeal. Dynamite Baits also make special carp
angler meatballs which can also be used as hookbaits.

The two tips I would give you with all meats is
that they are best fished without additional meat as free
offerings, and if you want to add more 'whoomph' fish
it in a PVA bag of crushed/crumbed boilies or pellets.
Secondly, all types of meat seem to be at their most
effective in the colder months so if the bog-standard
pineapple pop-up is not doing the trick then don't be
afraid to use a meat alternative.

Home-made Hook baits

Whilst the increase in popularity of carp fishing has meant
that all manner of baits are available 'off the shelf' it can

mean that your hookbait is often just the same as everyone else's. Just how many times will a carp make a mistake with a bog-standard pineapple or tutti-frutti hookbait when they've been done to death? Well they might still work on the right day but that's not always when you are there. By making your own hookbaits you can tweak them either slightly or massively as you wish. You don't have to have a yellow pineapple hookbait as the attractors may be fine but the colour may be deterring the carp. Why not make your own version in pink or white? You can add a degree of buoyancy if you wish with a cork ball or poly-pop. You can increase or decrease the attractor levels and so on. By making your own hookbaits you are not stepping into the

unknown but simply trying to swing things your way in the limited time you have.

Top An hour or two at home making alternative buoyancy hookbaits is time well spent.

Plastic Fantastic. I don't know why it works but it does.

Plastic Fantastic

Just like maggots the impact that plastic baits have had in the last few years has been tremendous. Originally it was the imitation sweetcorn but now companies like Enterprise Tackle have found a way of duplicating most things – in plastic. I have seen all sorts of theories as to why plastic hookbaits work but, to be honest, it's all theory and to me and you I hope the most important factor is simply that they do work. It may be the smell of the plastic, or it may be their resistance to nuisance fish, I don't care! I just know they work. When I fish maggots I tend to use an imitation one to form the Line Aligner and at least one on the hook to add buoyancy. With corn I like to fish a piece of imitation with two grains of the real stuff to balance it out. You know that it will not be nibbled away and come dawn you will have a hookbait still in position. By experimenting with these plastic baits it is possible to buy an extra bite or two so no matter how strange they may be in a logical sense believe me, they will catch you fish.

So there you have a number of changes you can make when what should work isn't working as quickly as it should be. In time you will know when to sit on your hands and when to experiment but now you have the ideas in front of you if you feel the need to make changes.

A double-figure common when I could only get bites on a bait tipped with yellow plastic corn.

Chapter Twenty Two
The Next Stage On

Although this book was written primarily for the short session angler fishing sessions of under 24 hours, I hope that any carp angler who reads it can use it to sharpen up their approach to the carp fishing time they have at their disposal. What I will assure you is if you follow and apply the information I have detailed your results will improve, and if they don't you know where to contact me. So you've followed the advice and things are going nicely... "Is that it?" you may end up asking yourself. Well no, of course it isn't, and although carp fishing is different things to different people, one thing I have noticed is if you stop going forwards you can end up going backwards. Now I am not for one minute telling you to fish more and more at the cost of anything else in your life but if carp fishing is important to you it is important to keep on top of it. I have friends who may in all likelihood be a lot more naturally gifted as anglers than I am but at the end of the day talent is only effective if you apply it. How many times have you heard the phrase 'a wasted talent'? Lots, I bet and I know it applies just as much to carp fishing as anything else.

To finish the book I want to give you some pointers on how to move on to the next level in carp fishing, how to improve your results and push yourself a little bit more each year. Nothing too difficult, but from lessons I have learnt by watching others succeed and fail, and I am sure these will help you improve your carp fishing even though you may never be able to fish anything other than short sessions. Remember that I too am probably in the same boat as you and with all that I have going on in my life, in all honesty, I get a lot less time to fish now than I did when I first started. It's not about the time you have but how you use that time.

Don't Take Time Out

Well I'd better clarify that really. Although it's fine to step back and look at what you are doing on these short sessions especially if things are not going well, there's a world of difference between taking a week or two off and taking six months or more off. The more you fish the more you learn unless you are simply going through the motions. If you take great chunks of the year off or pack it in every so often because something new catches your fancy then you will end up going well back in your learning curve. I see many lads pack it in or miss out great chunks of the year because they are too intense at times, have unrealistic expectations or don't have the necessary balance in their life where they can see carp fishing for what it is. Have another look at the chapter I wrote on getting your mind into gear and that may reinforce this point. You can't step it up a gear if you are not doing it.

You never know when the big fish will bite. I was tempted not to fish that night, but I did, and was rewarded with this stunning mirroor.

Carp Matches

Now I bet that has shocked a few of you! Although I am not in any way a competitive carp angler I certainly know that those who are can teach me a lot. Carp matches really do teach you to make the most of your time and from what I have seen the anglers who win these matches are not just competent match anglers, they are great carp anglers. I have fished some carp matches and qualified for the BCAC Final so I have seen first hand just how good these guys are. Names like Jarrett, Gawthorne, Jackson, Maker, O'Connor and so on. All great carp anglers, never mind match anglers, and they have that mindset to catch as many as they can as quickly as they can, often in a swim they don't want to be in. Sound familiar? Yes, that's an extreme version of the short session approach you and I have to deal with on a regular basis. Do yourself a favour and find out when the qualifiers are for the BCAC and go along to one – and maybe the final too if it is in your area. They take place from early April to late summer so it's an ideal time to see how these lads cope with short sessions. Because they are countrywide and usually on day ticket venues that you and I can fish it probably will be reflective of what we have to do anyway. It does not cost anything to watch and you can observe at close quarters just

The writings of others motivates me to try harder. Anglers like Peter Springate still motivate me to try harder each year.

how these anglers go about catching. From spodding to accurate groundbaiting, Zigs to long-range single baits, I guarantee you will come away inspired and informed and maybe even want to try it for yourselves.

Perfect Your Weaknesses

No angler is competent at all disciplines of carp fishing but the more you practise the better you will become. Once you find what works for you it is tempting to use that method to death, sometimes at the expense of other things. I know some anglers who are great at long-range casting but hopeless in the edge, or when fishing in weed. They are great at spodding but useless at stalking. Some are floater fishing gurus but don't have the mindset to do overnighters, and so on. Take a look at your fishing and what you are good and not good at. This requires you to be honest with yourself and not just to 'think' you can do everything well. I can do overnighters standing on my head,

will move in winter and can cast as far as needed, and so on. However, although I am competent at stalking and floater fishing the waters I have fished have never meant I needed to be anything other than competent. This year I have joined a water that responds to both so I will have to up my game. Even now I am getting my head round those disciplines and how I can build myself an edge on my short sessions. So after 25 years I still can very easily step up a gear if I have to... and I do!

Take time out to listen to advice. Here, my mate 'Big Bill Cottam' is entertaining a local fish-in audience.

Setting Targets

I am not really competitive when it comes to other carp anglers but when it comes to me versus the carp I am. When you have some experience under your belt it is possible to have some idea about what you expect to catch each year, or at each venue. What I have found is that setting myself a target can help me push myself even when time is limited. It might not be numbers, it could be size- or target-fish based. One of my friends Simon Crow is what I call a big-fish man and although he does catch plenty of fish, he spends a lot of the limited time he has concentrating on certain big fish when he thinks they are catchable. Although I am not necessarily a big-fish angler I do target one from time to time. When a fish, or some fish, get under your skin a short session angler can be as effective, sometimes even more so, than an angler who has more time at his disposal. Is there a big fish you really want to catch that you can spend time targeting? If there is then why not use your short sessions to target it rather than pursue numbers of fish? If you are learning to push yourself you will improve as an angler anyway, which you can utilise if you change your water next year. Singling out big fish will teach you a lot and may require you to up your game in many areas of your fishing. Maybe you will have to improve your observational skills, or your stalking abilities, casting and so on. The stepping up will improve you as an angler.

Think Long Term

Be inspired and learn from others. My friend Simon Crow is single-minded when in pursuit of a big fish, something I need to get my head round if I want to emulate his results.

As a carp angler you will have good and bad sessions, and good and bad years. If you are just living 'for the day' you can lose focus at times, and certainly perspective. Although I do try my hardest each time and it does hurt when I don't succeed, when I am in the Jeep going home I am usually looking forward to the next session, analysing where I went wrong and tuning up for the next one. If you can start to develop the long-term mindset failure on the day won't feel so bad and will simply mean you are one step closer to getting it right. Similarly, I know that when things are going right, in all likelihood, sooner or later things will go wrong. This has taught me to push myself hard on my multiple catch methods to milk it whilst I can because tomorrow those carp may be gone, that method old hat, and my window of opportunity closed. Same goes with waters. Yes I may well be happy with the ones I am on this year, and maybe next year, but what about the future? Do I need to get my name down for another water, or waters? No point in finding out that the ideal water for you is now full because you were too busy somewhere else. Step up your long-term vision for your own carp fishing future.

Conferences and Shows

Coming into contact with other carp anglers will teach you a lot no matter how good you are. Or should that be no matter how good you think you are!? Although I tend to fish mostly local waters having fished in places like Norfolk, Surrey, Kent and Hampshire I know that every water I have ever fished has taught me something. Not necessarily the water but the anglers fishing it. With limited time and finances it is not always possible to visit waters all over the country but you don't have to, I promise. One of the best ways to come into contact with other anglers rather than fishing all over the place is by attending conferences, slide shows and meetings. The people you meet and watch giving the talks may well fish different waters to you but how they approach their waters can be quite useful when it comes to you and your water. Whenever I watch anybody, or listen to anybody, I am always thinking what can I pinch from him to make my fishing easier? It could be how he deals with selecting big fish, his rigs, bait application and so on. I have yet to go to a talk that I have not learnt something from and I've been doing it for 25 years. The 5-Lakes Carpin' On show is probably the best way to do this. As well as the talks and forums, Mike Kavanagh and myself run the 'Rig and Bait Clinic' where anglers like Terry Hearn, Dave Lane, Kevin Nash and so on will show you how to tie their rigs and make their baits and so on. A book or DVD is one thing but seeing it being done live in front of you is better still. The inspiration and information you can pick up from such shows is essential if you want to step out of your comfort zone and step up a gear.

Everything I see and read inspires me to try harder. I'd had a hard day at work, but chickening out was not an option. I was glad I made the effort in the end!

So there you have it a number of ways that any short session carp angler can step up a gear and become more successful with the limited time they have available. Nothing too radical, nothing that involves you really spending more time at it, but just focussing at being better at what you do. Get all that right and I look forward to reading the books you write to inspire me. I certainly hope so!

Drop Me A Line

No book can ever hope to be all things to all anglers so as a very first in the world of carp books I am including an address where you can write to me and expect to get a reply tailored to your fishing. As a long-time carp angler myself I do know that no matter how good an article or chapter is, and no matter how easy it is to replicate the author's tactics and ideas, sometimes you would have liked to ask him or her 'What if I...' Well my friends now you can.

If any of you want any additional help, or are having problems with your carp fishing, then drop me a line and I will do my best to help, or find someone who can. Try to give me as much information as you can as the more I know about you and your carp fishing the more accurate my reply will be. So whether it's baits, rigs, tactics, or even just how to utilise the advice I have given in this book just drop me a line. All I ask is that you do include a stamp addressed envelope with at least one first class stamp on it. Every letter will be answered and although it may take a letter or two to solve your problem between us nothing is unsolvable.

You can write to me at the following address:

The Willows
Thorpe Lane
Thorpe In Balne
Doncaster
DN6 0DY

References

Tackle And Bait Manufacturers

Antbait
Morris Farm, Old Holbrook,
Horsham, West Sussex, RH12 4TW
www.antbait.co.uk

C and M Eyewear
Unit G3, Powerhub Business Centre,
Maidstone, Kent, ME16 0ST
www.rapideyewear.com

Daiwa Sports Limited
Netherton Industrial Estate, Wishaw,
Lanarkshire, Scotland, ML2 0EY
www.daiwasports.co.uk

Drennan/ESP
Bocardo Court, Temple Road,
Oxford, OX4 2EX
www.esp-carpgear.com

Dynamite Baits
Development Centre,
Fosse Way, Cotgrave,
Nottinghamshire, NG12 3HG
www.dynamitebaits.com

Enterprise Tackle
6 Darlington Close, Middlefield
Industrial Estate, Sandy,
Beds, SG19 1RW
www.enterprisetackle.co.uk

Fox UK
Fowler Road, Hainault Business Park,
Essex, IG6 3UT
www.foxint.com

Gardner Tackle
Unit 7, Quadrum Park, Old Portsmouth
Road, Guildford, Surrey, GU3 1LU
www.gardnertackle.co.uk

Heathrow Bait Services
Unit 9, Elmcott Farm, Great North
Road, Biggleswade, Beds, SG18 9BE
www.heathrowbaitservices.co.uk

Hinders Fishing Superstore
Manor Garden Centre,
Cheney Manor, Swindon, SN2 2QJ
www.hinders.co.uk

Korda
PO Box 6313, Basildon,
Essex, SS14 0HW
www.korda.co.uk

Kryston Advanced Angling,
Paragon Business Park, Chorley
New Road, Horwich, Bolton, BL6 6HG
www.kryston.com

Nash Tackle
PO Box 2061, Rayleigh,
Essex, SS6 9WQ
www.nashtackle.com

Nutrabaits
Units C1 and C2, Canklow Meadows
Industrial Estate, West Bawtry Road,
Rotherham, S60 2XL
www.nutrabaits.net

Optilabs
109 Stafford Road, Croydon, CR0 4NN
www.optilabs.com

Richworth Baits
Streamselect Limited,
Island Farm Avenue,
West Molesey, Surrey, KT8 2UZ
www.richworthbaits.com

Rollin' Baits
Unit 3C, Canklow Meadows
Industrial Estate, West Bawtry Road,
Rotherham, S60 2XL

TheTackle Box
251 Watling Street, Dartford,
Kent, DA2 6EG
www.tacklebox.co.uk

Wychwood
Units 8 and 9 Moons Park, Burnt
Meadow Road, North Moons Moat,
Redditch, Worcs, B98 9PA
www.wychwood-carp.co.uk

Publications

Crafty Carper
Angling Publications Limited,
Regent House, 101 Broadfield Road,
Sheffield, S8 0XH
www.anglingpublications.co.uk

Carpworld
Angling Publications Limited,
Regent House, 101 Broadfield Road,
Sheffield, S8 0XH
www.anglingpublications.co.uk

Carp Talk
Carp Fishing News, Newport,
East Yorkshire, HU15 2QG
www.carptalk-online.co.uk

Organisations

British Carp Study Group
www.bcsg.org.uk

Carp Society
Horseshoe Lake, Burford Road,
Lechlade, Glos, GL7 3QQ
www.thecarpsociety.com

ECHO
c/o Yateley Angling Centre,
16 The Parade, Yateley,
Hants, GU46 7UN
www.echo.co.uk

References

Other Books by Angling Publications Ltd:

Carp!
Tim Paisley 2002

Memories Of Carp
Tim Paisley 2004

The Ultimate Carp Rig Book
Martin Ford & Tim Paisley 2006

Another Romp With Carp
Albert Romp 2008

Carp Along The Way Volume 1
Rod Hutchinson 2008

Carp Along The Way Volume 2
Rod Hutchinson 2009

Just For The Record
Lee Jackson 2009

www.anglingpublications.co.uk